MW00643300

GOING
FAST
AND
FIXING
THINGS

GOING FAST AND FIXING THINGS

True Stories from the World's Most Popular DIY Repair Expert and Car Aficionado

RICH BENOIT

Creator of the Rich Rebuilds *YouTube channel*

and LISA ROGAK

New York Times *bestselling author*

hachette
BOOKS

NEW YORK

Jacket design by Amanda Kain
Jacket photograph by Scott Nobles
Jacket copyright © 2024 by Hachette Book Group, Inc.

Hachette Go, an imprint of Hachette Books

Hachette Book Group
1290 Avenue of the Americas
New York, NY 10104
HachetteGo.com
Facebook.com/HachetteGo
Instagram.com/HachetteGo

First Edition: June 2024

Published by Hachette Go, an imprint of Hachette Book Group, Inc. The Hachette Go name and logo is a trademark of the Hachette Book Group.

The Hachette Speakers Bureau provides a wide range of authors for speaking events. To find out more, go to hachettespeakersbureau.com or email HachetteSpeakers@hbgusa.com.

Hachette Go books may be purchased in bulk for business, educational, or promotional use. For information, please contact your local bookseller or Hachette Book Group Special Markets Department at: special.markets@ hbgusa.com.

The publisher is not responsible for websites (or their content) that are not owned by the publisher.

Print book interior design by Bart Dawson

Library of Congress Control Number: 2024931061

ISBNs: 978-0-306-83221-5 (hardcover); 978-0-306-83223-9 (ebook)

Printed in the United States of America

LSC-H

Printing 1, 2024

For my mother, who inspired my love for cars

If you're doing everything you can,
it's only a matter of time.
If you're not doing everything you can,
then just start.

—

RICH BENOIT

CONTENTS

INTRODUCTION   xiii

Chapter One
LIKE QUIET SEX   1

Chapter Two
MISSPENT YOUTH   19

Chapter Three
ESCAPING THE BARREL   37

Chapter Four
GAINING TRACTION   53

Chapter Five
THE LAND OF LOST TOYS   65

Chapter Six
HOW THE SAUSAGE GETS MADE   83

Chapter Seven
FIGHTING THE TESLA MONSTER   97

Chapter Eight
THE BACKLASH   111

Chapter Nine
JUMPING SHIP   125

Chapter Ten
DWB* 135

Chapter Eleven
ICE-T 149

Chapter Twelve
UNSOCIAL MEDIA 159

Chapter Thirteen
**EVERYTHING YOU EVER WANTED TO KNOW ABOUT
LEENDA BUT WERE AFRAID TO ASK** 173

Chapter Fourteen
HORSE SEX 187

Chapter Fifteen
GAME OVER 199

APPENDIX 217

ACKNOWLEDGMENTS 225

GOING
FAST
AND
FIXING
THINGS

INTRODUCTION

*C*oming to America was my mother's favorite movie.

She bought the videocassette when it first came out and she'd watch it again and again with her sisters, my aunts.

After all, they could relate. They had all immigrated to the United States from Trinidad and had to familiarize themselves with a whole new culture that didn't understand them.

I sat beside them on the couch, watching Eddie Murphy navigate through an unfamiliar, occasionally hostile world. I was only seven years old and most of the jokes went over my head, but I didn't care. I loved to hear my family laugh, and that's all that mattered.

One night, we all settled onto the couch for a repeat performance, but when my mom hit Play, nothing happened.

She ejected the blocky videocassette, turned the machine on and off, and smacked it on the side. She and my aunts tried a few other things, but nothing worked.

My aunt wrapped the cord around the machine and tucked it into the closet. I knew they didn't have the resources to fix it—back then, there were appliance repair shops on every corner—or buy another. They all worked multiple jobs to make ends meet, and watching goofy videos was one of the few times they were able to relax.

I hated to see them unhappy.

I wanted to be their hero.

"I'll fix it!" I announced.

They glanced at each other, then at me.

Even though I was only seven years old, I loved to take things apart, whether or not they were broken. I started with the fake Rolex (Folex) watches that my dad brought back from overseas business trips, and even though they were fake my dad always told me that having a nice watch makes a good impression. When he was at work, I'd sneak them out of his dresser so I could pry out all the springs and tiny screws. And when a Sharpie dried out, I cracked open the plastic case, soaked the felt strip in water, and taped the whole thing back up.

Of course, today I realize there's no way I could have fixed a VCR, but my mom and aunts liked to indulge me. I was one of those annoying kids who never stopped asking questions. How does this work? Why does it work this way and not that way? Where did it come from? I was a sponge, curious about everything.

Besides, when your seven-year-old kid says he can fix something, your expectations of success are probably hovering somewhere around zero.

Aw, he thinks he can fix it.

My aunt took the VCR out of the closet and set it on the kitchen table.

"Go fix it," she said, a big smile on her face.

I stared down at the VCR. Somewhere inside that metal box something was broken, and if I could figure out what it was, then Eddie Murphy could make them laugh again.

The cover was held on with four screws. Because I'd already taken apart transistor radios and boom boxes, I thought once I took out the screws, the top should just pop right off.

It did. But there were hundreds of pieces crammed into the small space: plastic nibs sticking out of the bottom, small metal cages with holes popped into them, a wide plastic ribbon that ran from one side of the box to the other. There were gear-toothed wheels that spun, and a green board with thin white lines and tiny silver-headed screws built in.

Somewhere in there was the reason we couldn't watch Eddie Murphy.

My pulse raced. This was *much* better than my father's watches, and, shoot, all these pieces did a lot more than just tell time! What did they all do? And how did they work together?

We lived in a small house in Mattapan, a mostly African American suburb of Boston. My mother had decorated the place like she was back in Trinidad, with lots of oranges and yellows and browns and a few steel drums propped against the wall. The house was always crammed with aunts, friends, husbands, and friends of friends who needed a place to crash for a while. My half brother even stayed with us before he left for the Marines.

It wasn't a quiet place.

As I undid screws and pulled out wires and cables, all the noise and chaos in the house—even the smell of curry and plantains that were always simmering away on the stove—faded into the background.

Thin rubber pulleys connected two circles, and if I yanked on the pulley both heads moved, but just in one direction.

A sticker with angry-looking letters: W-A-R-N-I-N-G: D-A-N-G-E-R-O-U-S V-O-L-T-A-G-E.

I unsnapped one piece from another. When I snapped it back into place, the *click* made me feel like I had accomplished something important.

An hour later, the case was empty and everything that had been inside it was now scattered across the floor. Now I can fix it! I started to put it back together, but there were so many pieces that I couldn't remember what went where.

But I wasn't worried, because I was learning something new.

When I had put everything back together, there were still a few screws and parts left over. I screwed the cover back into place and plugged it in. I pressed Play but nothing happened.

Eddie Murphy wasn't going to show up tonight. I shoved the VCR and extra parts under my bed.

I felt bad that I couldn't fix the VCR because I was disappointing my mom and aunts. But that sadness quickly faded because I learned how the VCR worked, and that was even more important because it meant that I could fix it for real the next time. Fun fact: there *was* no next time, since VCRs were already starting to be phased out.

It definitely taught me about failure, that not everything is peaches and roses.

My mom eventually bought a new VCR, but she never threw the old one away. Not only were people crammed into that small house, but things claimed a lot of space as well. Today they'd call it hoarding, but back then it was survival. My parents grew up on an island where it was hard to get anything, and they were poor. I don't mean poor by modern standards, like you live in a van down by the river. I mean *poor* poor: they didn't have running water, they bathed outside with a bucket and rainwater, and they went to the bathroom outside, in an *outhouse*. They also had dogs, but not the kind of dogs we have in America. You know how some owners need to put their dogs on a diet? Not there. These dogs were *hungry*, and they served a real purpose: they were hunting dogs.

Because my family didn't have much, they learned to make do with what they had. They never threw anything away because they never knew when it would come in handy.

Of course, the apple didn't fall far from the tree.

After the VCR, I looked around for other things to take apart, broken or not. If someone had a broken radio or toaster oven, they always knew who to give it to.

I've been taking things apart—and fixing them—ever since.

No one is more surprised than I am that I've made it this far. After all, I had so many strikes against me from the beginning.

I grew up in the hood.

My parents spent most of their time working, so I basically had to raise myself.

I became a father when I was a teenager.

Did I mention that I'm Black? Not sure if you saw the cover of the book...

And when it came time to follow my dream of becoming an auto mechanic straight out of high school, I was thwarted.

Today, I have a successful career on YouTube and am a landlord with multiple properties. I'm also a producer, actor, teacher, and business owner, and I have appeared on successful shows with A-list celebrities like Robert Downey Jr. More on that later.

I'm living proof that your life now doesn't have to be your life later.

My dad is probably one of the greatest storytellers that I know: he's funny, he's entertaining, and he's engaging. People would sit there, intently focused and laughing in all the right places.

And 93 percent of everything that came out of his mouth was made up.

But they were such good stories. I get 70 percent of my storytelling ability from him. The other 30 percent comes from watching great people perform.

It's no secret that I do love a good conspiracy theory. I fully admit that I regularly blur the lines of truth in my videos, so that viewers often don't know what's real and what's fake. And when I create these worlds, sometimes *I* don't even know what to believe anymore. It's kind of crazy, but at the same time, it's lots of fun. After all, how many people can live two lives at once?

What's more is that no one ever believes that I have children. In fact, many people think that I actually borrow someone else's kids to stand in for the ones who occasionally appear in my videos. Think about how that sounds: "Do you mind if I borrow your kid for one of my videos?"

I'm constantly thinking of how I can create and live new stories, and because I've created a world that looks and sounds real, people either think I live in a castle in the sky or that I'm homeless, and all because I have a YouTube channel that tells you how I fix cars. And I guess my biggest thing is entertainment. What does it matter if it's real or not?

Why do people want to know? Do they want to model themselves after me? Oh no, please, anything but that. Or do they think they know me based on my videos? Do they think we're friends? Sometimes someone will come up to me and say, "Hi, Rich," like I'm a long-lost friend and just start talking. I have no idea who they are, but because I come across as so friendly and approachable in my videos, they figure I'm like that in real life too. I am, but mostly with people I know. Otherwise, it gets real weird really fast. The last post I need on Reddit is "Yeah, that *Rich Rebuilds* guy, what a jerk."

I make videos because I want to entertain people and I hope they learn something in the process. That's it. And from the response I've gotten over the years, I've succeeded. So if that's the case, then the reality isn't so important, right? But it feels like people want to latch onto something, and some see me as a hero or a person they could look up to.

I wrote this book so I could give people a bit more perspective on my own life. After all, there's a lot of mystery about who I am.

Many viewers like to take bits and pieces of information about me and then build a whole new story around it. I get a huge kick out of people wondering what my deal is. You wouldn't believe the hours I spend just belly laughing at people who are trying to figure out my life in the Comments section. One time a guy essentially wrote a whole thesis about my life: *Well, Rich got divorced seven years ago, and if you look carefully, he's not wearing his wedding ring*—and on and on as he built a highly entertaining story. And because he went into such detail, other viewers thought he must be an insider who had the real scoop, and then they believed him too. I'm not going to lie: even *I* believed it. He was actually pretty close on a few things.

Why are they so invested in my private life? Sometimes I think it's because they're not happy in their own relationships, and they think that if I'm no longer married, then maybe they shouldn't be either. I swear that the people who do this could have pretty successful careers doing detective work, and here they are giving their gift away for free.

Sometimes Leenda and I call each other to share stories about how crazy all this is, and no, we're not in a relationship. But it is very entertaining.

Over the course of writing this book, I've been thinking deeper about myself and what I really want in life. Maybe there's a good reason I'm doing this, a much deeper reason. Maybe I'm not happy with my current reality, or maybe I think I'm capable of more. Maybe I create these scenarios to also live in that space, to ask myself, "Okay, what's *this* like? Can I do *this*?"

I'm hoping that you can come away with a good chuckle, and I also want to let you know in the most long-winded way possible that your life can change. After all, I thought I was destined for failure: I had a kid, got divorced, and was paying child support all before I was old enough to buy a beer. Because of this, it's important for me to let people know that your life now doesn't have to be your life later, because as things turned out for me, that wasn't the case at all. Today, my life couldn't be better.

I also want to give my fans a behind-the-scenes look at my success in the hope that I can inspire people. I'll talk about my struggles and how it doesn't matter what you have—somewhere along the line, life is going to punch you in the face and you're going to struggle. I wish I had a dollar for every night I've spent screaming into the void.

Some say life is like a box of chocolates: you never know what you are going to get, but at least you know you're going to get chocolate, not a Madagascar hissing cockroach. But I'd say it's more like the Oregon Trail, filled with misery and dysentery, but with some luck and good preparation, you may make it to Idaho.

Writing this book changed me because it challenged me. Digging up my life story uncovered memories and areas of my life that I haven't thought about in decades. It also sparked a new area of creativity for me since I had to learn how to tell a story without video, just words.

When I was a kid, my mom liked to tell me, "Richie, you have a gift. You weren't blessed with looks, but damn, you're entertaining."

YouTube combines everything I've ever wanted to do because I've always wanted to be a teacher. I was always the class clown, and it's kind of what I do now. I get real joy from seeing others be happy.

All it took was a salvaged flood car that everyone else had given up for dead to bring all this to light.

CHAPTER ONE

LIKE QUIET SEX

When my buddy Chad showed up in my driveway in a brand-new Tesla one day in 2014 and told me to get in, I almost sent him packing.

My friends teased me that I only drove cars that middle-aged white men loved, because I had long been a fan of muscle cars like the Camaro and pretty much anything with a Hemi in it. Maybe, but it didn't bother me in the least. If you want to have fun driving a car, it has to make lots of noise and go fast. Otherwise, why bother?

Chad was a fellow car nut and had been working at Tesla as a mechanic for a few years. He had long raved about the brand, but I had tuned him out. In my mind, electric cars were for tree huggers and vegans. Hybrids like the Toyota Prius were starting to make headway, but few electric vehicles were produced in any quantity aside from the Chevy Volt and the Nissan Leaf, which was just about the ugliest car ever made aside from the Pontiac Aztek. I'd rather ride a penny-farthing bike than be seen in a Nissan Leaf. Besides, EVs back then were woefully underpowered and could maybe manage a range of one hundred miles on a good day.

But Chad wouldn't take no for an answer. He opened the door of the Model S on loan from his boss and I climbed into the driver's seat. "How do you start this thing?" I asked.

"It's already running," he replied.

It is? Huh. I put it into reverse to back out of the driveway. Still no noise. Weird.

I shifted into drive and hit the accelerator. The car lurched forward and the power pushed me back in my seat even more than when I floored my beloved Corvette.

Okay, that checked off one box. But it was still too quiet. Eerily so.

It was a huge disconnect: the car had incredible torque and was so fast off the line—from zero to sixty in 4.2 seconds, I'd later learn—but it made no noise. How could that be? I pushed my confusion aside and relaxed into the experience. Quiet *and* power. Maybe this is what driving a stealth bomber was like. Maybe you really could have that much fun in total silence. It was like quiet sex: quiet, but still fun.

I don't remember where we went or what we talked about, but when Chad and I landed back in my driveway fifteen minutes later, I knew that my life had permanently changed. There was BT (Before Tesla) and AT (After Tesla).

I wanted one, and I wanted one *now*. I've bought a lot of cars in my life and have often stretched to buy more car than my budget—or wife—was comfortable with. But motor oil ran through my veins, and I'd easily spent tens of thousands of dollars on cars I shouldn't have bought up to that point.

I loved tinkering with them as well. To me, there was nothing better than taking apart a car to see how it worked and then putting it back together to make it work even better. It made me feel complete, calm. Whenever I was upset or needed to cool my jets, I'd head into the garage to wrestle with an exhaust manifold or brake cylinder, emerging hours later triumphantly flailing my bloodied knuckles like I had just won a boxing match.

And whatever had been bothering me had faded into the background.

I reluctantly pulled myself out of the driver's seat and asked Chad how much it cost.

"Close to six figures for a performance model," he replied.

So much for my new AT life. No way could I afford that kind of money for a car on my salary as an IT help specialist at a major Boston financial firm. Plus, I wasn't selling my beloved Corvette Z06 for *that*.

After I stood in the driveway watching Chad pull away, I dragged myself into the garage to drown my sorrows in my current project, a Jeep Grand Cherokee SRT8 with 420 horsepower. When I'd bought it a few months earlier, it was a shiny new toy I couldn't wait to get my hands on. Now, in my post-Tesla haze, it looked boring and drab.

I couldn't bring myself to work on the Jeep, so I went inside to scroll through the car sites to see if Chad was wrong, or to torture myself.

Or both.

The first Tesla model—the Roadster—came out in 2008 and only 2,450 were sold. The Model S—Chad's car—started production in 2012, and only seventy thousand Teslas had been sold by then. By contrast, in 2014, Ford sold seventy thousand vehicles about every thirty-four days. That meant Tesla prices would likely remain high for the foreseeable future, which the car sites confirmed for me. As I scrolled, looking for a low-priced unicorn, a light bulb went off. I didn't come from money and I've always been a cheapskate. In fact, I've only bought one new car in my lifetime. Why buy new when used is usually just as good and a lot cheaper? That's how I grew up, and it ran deep.

Maybe there were salvage Teslas out there, ones I could actually afford. Salvage cars scare away most car buyers, but they can be a good deal for someone who loves to tinker, and I've bought some great cars at a fraction of the cost. Salvage cars are vehicles that were in accidents or other disasters that insurance companies have deemed too expensive and not feasible to repair. I switched over to the salvage sites and found a 2012 Model S in New Jersey that had been in a flood, also something that scares most car buyers. I googled "Tesla" and "flood" and watched several interviews where CEO Elon Musk said that a Tesla could be submerged in water for some time without causing any lasting harm.

Oh, Elon, you sweet summer child...

The car cost $14,000, half of what was in my savings account and around one-fifth of the car's original cost. I had to run it by my wife first. I told her what I wanted to do and how I felt while driving it. We'd been together for almost a decade at that point, and she knew that my car jonesing ran deep. She asked a few questions, but she definitely got it.

"Okay, go do your thing."

I am a lucky man.

That kind of trust is exactly what is needed to fix a car. After all, I'm not a trained mechanic and have learned to repair cars through a combination of applying skills learned elsewhere and a lot of dumb luck.

Despite her go-ahead, I was still pretty nervous. At the time, it was one of the largest gambles I'd ever taken. And because I didn't know how working on an electric car was different from a gas vehicle, I had no idea what I was in for. But sometimes you just have to say, *Hey, look, I have these two pennies. I'm gonna knock them together and see what happens.*

After I paid for the car, I arranged for a towing company to deliver it. Then I headed to the supermarket to buy a few bags of rice. After all, it works for cell phones, why not a Tesla?

My first *Oh, shit* moment came when the tow driver called a few weeks later.

"Hey, man, you didn't tell me it didn't run or drive," he said. "And there's no key. How am I supposed to get into the car, forget about starting it?" I looked like I had lost all my Sonic rings like in the video game.

I had no clue. My Tesla experience had lasted all of fifteen minutes, and that car was already running when I got in.

Since the car was dead—and because there was no key—it had to be loaded onto the flatbed with a massive forklift. When the driver showed up in my driveway, we jacked up the car while it was still on the trailer, slid a tow dolly under each tire, and managed to wheel the car down the ramp without killing anyone. It took every ounce of strength to maneuver the car into the garage. The Tesla Model S is about the size of an Audi A6 but weighs as much as a Lincoln Navigator, about five thousand pounds. The driver left, shaking his head at the poor sucker who bought this loser of a car.

Now *I* had to be the one to figure out how to get into the car with no key or power. When I smashed the window, the stench made me gag and run outside. It smelled like a fermented onion smoothie.

I must admit that right then part of me wanted to turn back the clock to the moment before my first ride in a Tesla, or at least to the last seconds before I entered the winning bid for the car. I felt like I'd been duped. While I knew it was a flood car, I didn't know it was *salt* water. Salt water is extremely caustic, and I'd soon discover that all the electronic and battery modules were completely corroded. For a graphic look, watch "Tesla Model S Corroded Battery Modules," my very first YouTube video posted back on March 10, 2016, in which I use one of my favorite mechanical tools, a plastic butter knife.

Of course, the car was totally unresponsive and nothing worked. I'd later learn that it had been submerged in water during Superstorm Sandy in 2012 for several days, not the quick dip that Musk had said not to worry about.

As I stared at the reeking puddle of salt water in the back seat, two things came to mind. Number one was my wife saying the dreaded words, "I told you so." Number two was the prospect of losing the $14,000 I'd spent, since it would be close to impossible to sell a salt-water-flooded car.

I breathed through my mouth so I wouldn't retch from the pungent smell of what I would describe as a warm turtle tank. I relaxed a little, because I've tackled basket-case cars before. I thought of the moment that always comes: the sweet spot while working on a car that I've put my whole heart and soul into, when I *know* it's going to work despite the weeks of uncertainty. Most of the time this feeling comes when I'm 99 percent of the way done. But even though I'd never worked on an electric car before—let alone one drowned in salt water—I knew I would eventually reach that sweet spot. And perhaps that sweet spot was selling the car and cutting my losses.

So I dove in.

I am happiest when I'm taking something apart because that means I'm learning something new. Flood car or not, the Tesla was a complete mystery, but how hard could it be? There were no hoses to clamp off or push out of the way, and I didn't have to worry about splashing gasoline or oil onto my shoes.

I name most of my cars. I decided that this car should be named after a character who starts out as a damsel in distress but who eventually grows into a strong, powerful woman.

Wishful thinking, I know.

I christened her Dolores, after the character on the TV show *Westworld* who follows that exact trajectory. Funnily enough, I stopped watching *Westworld* immediately after I started to work on Dolores.

I studied the architecture of the car as I loosened nuts and bolts, tucking them into plastic bags and using a notebook to keep track of where they came from. The sheer beauty of a Tesla is its simplicity. It's just wires, semiconductors, a battery, and a motor.

This car does so much with so little. Over the next few days, I fell in love with it even more.

Unfortunately, the calm didn't last.

I needed parts.

After I took the car apart, I was left with a chassis. I needed an interior and a complete electronic system.

I made a list of the parts I needed and called the nearest Tesla service center. I told the rep I needed a battery, a motor, and seats, and I gave him the VIN.

After a few keystrokes, he came back on the line. "The car was in a flood and was totaled by the insurance company, so I can't sell you any parts."

Jazz music stops

Wait, what? Over the many years that I'd been working on cars, every auto parts store, junkyard, or online dealer had been thrilled to sell me used or new parts. In fact, I usually get a volume discount because I buy so many.

Maybe the rep hadn't had enough coffee that morning or was just cranky, so I hung up and called a different service center. This time, the rep actually took the time to explain why they don't sell parts to people like me.

"We don't want people fixing our cars because we're the only ones that can fix them, so you'll have to buy a new car if you want one that works," he said, and he transferred me to the sales department.

When I pried my jaw off the floor, I dialed a third. This time, the rep actually laughed in my ear.

I was trying to play pool with a rope.

I hung up. Something wasn't right. In 2012, the Massachusetts state legislature passed the Right to Repair initiative, which requires automotive manufacturers to provide consumers with the same repair and diagnostic information they give to dealerships and mechanics throughout the state. But then I read the fine print: the law only applies to manufacturers that have dealerships in the state, and Tesla doesn't have any because customers order their vehicles online, not in person. The company refused to sell parts not only to people who owned salvage vehicles but also to those whose cars were out of warranty, since Tesla obviously made more money selling a new car than selling parts. Not only that, but the company was so new that it didn't even *have* the parts to sell. They were busy making cars, not extra parts. I get it, but still...

Where was I going to get the parts I needed? Teslas were still too rare to be found in junkyards. I asked Chad if he could help, but as an employee of the company his hands were tied.

In retrospect, maybe I shouldn't have named the car Dolores. In addition to being the name of the protagonist in *Westworld*, Dolores means "pain" or "sad" in Spanish, which would be my mood for the foreseeable future when it came to the Tesla.

I thought there must be other people in the same boat, so I found an online forum for Tesla owners who worked on their own cars. Back then, there were no online groups like there are today on Facebook, where you can associate names with faces and if some jerk makes a comment you don't like, you can see his family and friends. In those days, you pretty much typed text into a box and that was it.

I also started a Facebook page where Tesla owners could buy, sell, or trade parts. That generated a few parts, but not the ones I actually needed. Still, I didn't know when I'd find them again so I grabbed what I could, because in addition to being a cheapskate, hoarding runs deep in my family.

To create an account on the forum, I needed an avatar. My sense of humor has always been a bit warped, so I chose "Hide the Pain Harold," an internet meme based on a photo of a white man in his seventies with a really awkward look on his face, like he has serious gas pains. I thought it was pretty funny, but it was also an attempt to mask who I was. As a Black man, I was familiar with how a large chunk of the world viewed me, and I wanted to keep the focus on cars.

At first, I asked for general advice and where to find used parts. But I also posted about some work-arounds I'd discovered, and soon people were asking me questions about my project. It was easier to show what I was describing instead of typing the answers, so I started uploading short videos.

Back then, there weren't a lot of people who were willing to explore the car like I was. So when I posted videos that showed the car completely torn apart, I got a lot of traction because no one had ever seen the inside of these cars before.

The videos were taking up too much space on my phone, and Carl Hewitt, a fellow forum member, reached out and suggested that I start making short-form videos for the world to see. I did just that, creating a YouTube account so I could upload them and free up some space. I called the channel *CarGuru*, and Tesla drivers who weren't on the forum soon found it and subscribed. I posted new videos both to the forum and to YouTube.

I was accidentally turning into some kind of Tesla expert, at least in one small corner of the internet. Apparently, many people thought I *was* Hide the Pain Harold, because one day all hell broke loose on the forum when I posted a video that accidentally showed a brief flash of my hand. In minutes, the racists came out of the woodwork, leaving comments on all my threads, and I'll leave it to you to imagine what they said. The moderators deleted them as soon as they appeared, but it turned into one big game of Whac-A-Mole. One side effect was that the members who were turned off by the FB forum switched to my YouTube channel instead.

I'd be lying if I said I've never experienced racism in my life, of course, but I've always taken it in stride. I've never been an Angry Black Man, and I wasn't going to start now. Some might see my worldview as a weakness, but I always like to give people the benefit of the doubt. Always. This has backfired on me numerous times throughout the years, but it's better than walking around angry at the world.

Instead, I tell myself that people act like this because they personally don't know anyone who fits my description. I've always considered it to be my job to prove them wrong. Back in elementary school—I was the only Black kid in my school for years—I realized that the only previous exposure that my class-mates had to Black people was on TV and in movies, which back in the '80s and '90s didn't tend to paint us in the best light: *New Jack City, Boyz n the Hood, Menace II Society*...the list goes on, but hey, they made money. I've always made it my personal mission to prove to people that we aren't always how you think we are.

The best thing for me to do was to focus on the job at hand: bringing a destroyed Tesla back to life.

When I started working on Dolores, it felt like I was working on an alien spacecraft, since I had no documentation or manuals. I found some half-baked guides online on how to do minor repairs, but nothing covered anything remotely close to bring-ing a car back from the dead. It felt like I had to learn a com-pletely new language, though a lot of the same methods from working on gas cars still applied. Dolores had brakes, brake calipers, and brake lines, so some of the parts were similar, but the method of propulsion was the polar opposite: instead of a gas engine driving power to the transmission, a battery pack directed power to the electric controller and then to the electric motor itself.

Some of the parts were also radically different in other ways. As I took Dolores apart, I made a surprising discovery: In the early Teslas, some of the parts actually came from other manufacturers. For instance, the steering rack was either from Mercedes or Land Rover, while the window switches, steering column, and turn signal stalks were all Mercedes parts. It's almost like they were sticking their hands in various parts bins to assemble a vehicle.

I'd swear that some of those early cars were held together with wood screws from Home Depot…and dude, *I would know.* Some of my own fixes were jerry-rigged, using every-thing from nuts and bolts to zip ties.

If you work on an old-school muscle car, like a Camaro or Corvette, for three days and follow all the basic rules of automotive repair, it'll eventually work. For instance, if you swap an old drive motor with a new one, as long as it's getting fuel and spark, it'll fire. But if you're working on that car after three days and it still doesn't work, then it's 100 percent your fault.

With Dolores, those rules went out the window. You can work on a Tesla for three, even five days and follow all the basic rules of automotive detective work, and if it still doesn't work, then it's the car's fault, because the car is primarily software.

Without a manual or any kind of documentation—which Tesla wouldn't distribute to non–Tesla employees—I was flying blind.

I realized I could solve a whole lot of my problems if I had another Tesla that was wrecked in all the ways Dolores was not. I found a salvaged Model S online with an intact interior and drivetrain that cost $14,000, which would clear out the rest of my savings account.

I passed it by my wife, fully expecting her to turn me down. But she just asked one question: "Do you think you could fix this thing?"

"Yes."

"Okay, then."

Like I said, I'm a lucky man.

When the car arrived in my driveway, I named it Slim Shady and got to work.

I quickly discovered that having a parts car was even better than having a manual. When I was taking the various components in Dolores apart, I had no idea how to put them back together. I kept notes and labeled the baggies I put them in, but my most frequent question was always *Where the hell does this thing go?*

With Slim Shady, the answers were very clear, and my progress on the car sped up exponentially. I'd essentially spent $14,000 on a repair manual, but it was worth every penny. I literally transferred every nut, bolt, and screw from one car to another. I didn't have room to keep two cars in the garage, so I stored Slim Shady at a friend's salvage yard about a ninety-minute drive away. I'd head there at night after work, take the parts I needed off the car, and then drive back, which made for some very long days . . . and nights.

The bad thing about a Tesla is that, with four hundred volts of electricity packed into the floor of the vehicle, the car has the potential to kill you at any given point in time.

Of course, the same could be said for a gas-powered car. After all, in order to get your car to move down the road, a steady stream of gasoline needs to run through a gas line under the rear seat—where your kids are probably sitting—to the front of the vehicle, where it is shot into a chamber, which creates a small explosion.

I'm not saying that one is safer or riskier than the other— they both have advantages and disadvantages—but a gas engine is a lot less dangerous than an electric car when it's turned off, because with a gas tank, you'd have to really screw up to blow up that car and any humans in it. You'd have to beat the crap out of the gas tank or punch a hole in it and then set fire to it on purpose.

With an electric car, no matter how you shake it, there are still four hundred volts coursing through that battery pack. One time, I had to pull all the fuses and couldn't shut off the power. So I slipped on a pair of lineman gloves, and while surrounded by small puddles of salt water I pulled the fuses. There was still a ton of electricity back there, and I could have died.

After spending almost a year of my life trying to make one good car from two bad ones, flying blind the entire time, the moment had finally arrived.

It was time to take Dolores out for a spin.

I almost didn't want to. After all, I'd been waiting for this for an incredibly long time. There was a lot of work leading up to this moment, not to mention a lot of money and too many sleepless nights to count.

But if it worked, it would totally rectify my inability to fix a VCR when I was seven years old.

WHAT A TOOL

When I started working on Dolores, I had very limited experience working on cars. I wasn't a mechanic, nor did I have the proper tools to *be* a mechanic. I got my first tool set—sockets, wrenches, drills, all that stuff—when I was working on my Dodge Neon SRT.

I needed to remove trim pieces from Dolores, and not only did I not have a trim removal tool but I didn't even know that such a thing existed. So I asked myself, *What's flat and can get into small spaces to pop off trim without marking up the doors?* A butter knife. Turns out, it was perfect. It also worked pretty good as a flathead screwdriver.

When I had to work on Dolores's batteries, I switched to a pink plastic knife, which I used in my very first YouTube video. It worked so well scraping off battery corrosion that I purchased a whole package of them just to have around.

When it comes to hammers, anything hard can be a hammer. Back then, the "hammer" I reached for most was a drill battery: it's short, compact, and easy to swing. At $200, it was expensive, but that's what was lying around. Shockingly, I never punctured one in all the time I've been rebuilding cars, and besides, where are you going to find something that broad to smack a bolt in?

CHAPTER TWO

MISSPENT YOUTH

I grew up in Mattapan, a Boston neighborhood that was pretty tough. I went to St. Mary's Catholic school in neighboring Milton, a wealthy town by comparison. My mother, father, two aunts, a live-in babysitter, and I all lived in a nine-hundred-square-foot, two-bedroom ranch with a tiny apartment in the basement, with various relatives and friends frequently passing through. Since then, I've seen RVs that are bigger than that house.

All the adults worked long hours. My mom was a hustler and worked several jobs, including one as a home health aide and another selling candy, newspapers, and coffee at a newsstand in a Boston subway station, while my father worked as an electrical engineer at companies like Varian and Honeywell, just to name a couple.

I was a latchkey kid, so I always came home to an empty house. The adults would show up hours later, and they all assumed I could take care of myself. "Are you good? You know where the food is. If you need something, just figure it out."

I was a happy kid and loved to play with my friends in the street. We'd play tag and hide-and-seek until the streetlights came on. Then we'd go over to each other's houses and hang out and play video games and talk about the girls we liked. We were preteens, little men and women trying to figure each other out and just starting to think about how to navigate life. The kids in that neighborhood were my first real friends, and back then, before cell phones and the internet, we had the chance to actually be kids.

I loved being home by myself because I could puzzle out how something worked. After I finished my homework, I had all the time in the world, plus I was unsupervised. I would take things apart—everything from the toaster oven to a ball-point pen—so I could learn how they worked. I was also pretty hyperactive as a kid, and my report cards and progress reports were littered with comments like "never sits still," "has limited attention span," and "Richie is like lightning." The only time I was able to calm down was when I was taking something apart or putting it back together, or trying to. I could sit for hours tinkering with something, poking its innards and pulling out wires to see what made it tick.

In grade school, my friends were mostly white, but I had a couple of Black friends who sometimes told me that I sounded too white. If I wanted more Black people to talk to me, I had to sound more Black. So I did that, but then my white friends would start to look at me funny, so I'd switch back.

Friends on both sides called me Carlton after Will Smith's younger cousin in *The Fresh Prince of Bel-Air*. Carlton was Black, but he acted white. He wore sweaters and slacks and he liked to listen to Tom Jones, all things that were normal in white culture back then. I always thought my identity shouldn't be determined by what I liked. I was into comic books and Legos and taking things apart, but I also liked rap music and MTV, and there was nothing wrong with that.

I straddled both worlds in high school, and I still do that today. At the end of the day, I know my core audience.

My mom and dad had both immigrated from Trinidad and Tobago, and I spent most summers in Trinidad with my mom's family. I played with my cousins, went fishing and caught crabs, and watched monkeys swing from trees while my family caught and ate armadillos. It was the total opposite of living in Boston, and I was utterly free. I was such a sponge; by the end of the summer, I was talking in my parents' native cadence, like a Trini.

When I got back home, my parents and aunts understood me, but no one else could. When I said "three," it came out *tree*. My teachers signed me up for speech therapy classes so I could revert back to speaking the way I did before. This is why I don't have a Trinidadian accent: I was reprogrammed at a young age.

My parents never married. To me, that was completely normal; it was what I knew. When you're a kid, your world is small and confined to your own interests. But when I was in fifth grade, my parents split up and my father moved to Salem, Massachusetts, which was about an hour away. Occasionally, he'd stay with us for a few days before going back to his house. Again, to me, this was completely normal.

In addition to his job, my father owned a couple of rental properties, and he'd drag me along to work on his houses, painting, putting up Sheetrock, and swapping out the heating system. My father had no business fixing homes or doing any kind of general contractor work, but he hated paying for something he thought he could do himself. I hated it because it felt too much like a job. I couldn't wait to go back to Mattapan and be with my mom and my aunts.

My mom worked incredibly hard because she wanted to have nice things. She loved cars, and during my childhood she drove a Buick Riviera, a Pontiac Firebird, and a Chevy Blazer at various times, always from General Motors. I later found out that she had always wanted a Corvette, and at one point she had saved up enough money to buy one, but then she discovered she was pregnant with me, so that dream went out the window. That's why I've always been big into GM, because that's what my mother had and it was what I grew up with.

My passion for taking things apart to see how they worked had expanded by my early teens, when I naturally gravitated to cars. I had run out of things in the house to take apart, so one day I turned to her Geo Prizm. Back in the early 1990s, if you didn't have a lot of money to spend on a car, you bought a Prizm, also a GM car. The car was as good as mine, since my mother had promised I'd get it when I turned sixteen.

I bought some terrible aftermarket speakers from the RadioShack down the street and installed them in her car without her finding out. Then I taught myself how to back out of the driveway and practiced my parking skills on the street. Late at night, I'd sneak out and drive the car around the block.

I was all of eleven.

Since I was getting away with driving my mother's car, I started to push the envelope in other ways, mostly with my friends. I had always been a good student, but I had started to slack off on my schoolwork and was staying out late on school nights. Plus, I was sassing my mom and my aunts, believing that I knew better than they did.

After I finished seventh grade, I left for Trinidad for the summer as usual. A few days before I flew home, my mom called me and cut to the chase.

"When you come back, you will not live with me anymore," she said. "You're going to live with your dad."

She and her sisters couldn't handle me anymore, and they thought that having a male influence would help rein me in. I couldn't believe it. I begged and pleaded and cried, but she wouldn't change her mind. When I got off the plane at Logan, my father picked me up instead of my mother.

The dildo of consequence rarely arrives lubed.

I had returned to a completely different world.

In Salem, I had to start from scratch.

In Catholic school, I was one of only a handful of Black kids. In Salem, the school was extremely diverse when I started eighth grade, and it was actually a bit of a culture shock.

There were also lots of cliques and different groups. Where did I fit in? And how should I act in order to fit in? I wanted to be with the cool kids, but I also wanted to be smart, to hang out with the nerds.

I decided that the only way to survive was to get along with absolutely everyone, so I joined the physics team, the science team, and the debate team to fit in with the nerds, and I played tennis to fit in with the jocks—though I later found out that the jocks were not, in fact, on the tennis team. To fit in with the cool kids, I walked like them, talked like them, and tried to dress like them. I would wear my mother's gold jewelry to school and to parties. I was one of the beautiful people. Honestly, I was more of a hybrid, but I played both parts exceedingly well.

The culture shock of a new school was hard enough, but the bigger problem was my father, since we didn't really get along. His skill set for dealing with me consisted of judgment and continuous disappointment. We didn't fight, but he was the opposite of my mom: very businesslike with very little nurturing. His goal was to turn me into a man: *I'll teach you, and you'll learn.* My dad's house was also deathly quiet, totally different from my mother's chaotic house. His idea of fun was to look for junk at junkyards and shop at Building #19, a closeout chain store filled with expired food and clothing that had gone out of style a couple of years before.

His mission was to ensure that we looked like we lived below the poverty line, and he largely succeeded.

I felt so isolated and depressed. I didn't want to live with him. I missed my friends, and I hated Salem.

When I started living with my father, I had no idea how to dress myself.

At Catholic school we all dressed alike; it was uniforms every day. On the weekends, my mom spoiled the hell outta me, buying me brand-name clothing: hats, jeans, sneakers. Plus, everything matched.

Image was everything in my new school, and kids sorted themselves into groups according to what they wore. When I moved in with my dad, we bought my clothes and sneakers at Building #19, which I knew would instantly ostracize me. I looked like a medieval peasant.

But I knew how to improvise from nothing. Back in Catholic school, we sang a little jingle that went "Reduce, reuse, recycle." This had been news to some of my classmates, but to me it was old hat. My parents never threw anything out. *Never.* After all, they grew up on a small, impoverished island where things were expensive and hard to source. My father had lots of junk stored in the basements of his rental apartments—everything from broken stoves to mangled fencing—that he might need someday.

In my new school, I wanted to be accepted by both the nerds and the cool kids who wore brand-name clothes. I didn't want to be seen as someone who couldn't afford that lifestyle. Back then, if you wore a Nautica jacket or shirt, you were the shit. A few weeks after classes started, I found a shirt on top of a trash can. It was oily, stained, and faded yellow.

But it was a Nautica.

I made sure that no one was looking as I stuffed it into my backpack. At home, I carefully cut out the logo and taped it to one of my button-up collared shirts. I wore it to school the next day and felt like a million bucks. I couldn't tell if my classmates treated me differently, but *I* felt different, and that was all that mattered.

I couldn't wear the same shirt every day, so I went to Marshalls to look for the cheapest Nautica I could find. Even though Marshalls was a discount department store, the adult shirts were still too expensive. I wandered over to the children's department and realized that kids' clothing was significantly cheaper. So I bought a couple of Nautica shirts for infants, cut out the logos, and taped them on my adult-size no-brand shirts from Building #19.

One day, a friend got suspicious and asked to see the inside tag. I made up some story about why I couldn't show it, but I knew I wouldn't be able to get away with it for long. So I came up with another plan.

When I was visiting my mom, I headed for Filene's Basement in Downtown Crossing in Boston. Filene's Basement was a department store madhouse filled with discounted clothes that hadn't sold at the regular full-priced Filene's store down the street. The Basement was a free-for-all where customers regularly got into fistfights over a pair of designer jeans at 75 percent off the list price.

I picked out a few shirts and pants and headed for the dressing room. They fit, so I walked around the whole store with them, pretending like I was shopping. I glanced at the door a few times. No one was looking in bags or checking tags, and the cashiers looked as harried as the customers.

I noticed that a guy with a mustache kept looking at me, but back then I didn't understand that security doesn't necessarily stand at the door wearing a uniform or hat. So I walked out of the store with the clothes and was heading upstairs when the guy with the mustache grabbed my arm and told me to come with him.

"Why?"

"You're shoplifting."

There was nothing that I could say. He brought me to the shoplifter holding room. Apparently, it happens so much that there's a separate room for it.

I. Was. Terrified.

Thankfully, he decided not to press charges because they'd never seen me in the store before, but I'd be banned for life from the store. And he had to call my mother.

That's a day I will never forget. As he told her why he was calling, I heard her scream from across the room.

"Not my son, not my son." Over and over.

She left work early to pick me up and sobbed the entire way back on the train. "How could you do this to me, when I give you everything?" I felt bad because she was crying like I had hurt her, and people kept looking at me, trying to figure out what I had done.

Then, I had to tell my father.

The belt felt a little bit different that day.

I've never thought about why I shoplifted. I don't know if I was being rebellious. I don't know if I felt bad for my mom and thought that she shouldn't have to pay for everything for me, or if I was mad at her because I had to live with my dad.

I still wanted brand-name clothing, but now I knew I had to pay for it, so I got a job as a cashier in a grocery store where I'd make five bucks an hour.

My plan was pretty simple. In my mind, a twenty-five-dollar Nike T-shirt was equal to five hours of work, and two weeks of work would pay for a pair of Jordans. But when my first paycheck arrived, I learned about the crushing reality of taxes. I couldn't afford the shirt; forget about the Jordans.

One day, a kid I went to high school with came through my checkout line. I knew he had gotten his girlfriend pregnant and that they had a kid together. He had stayed in school, but based on the look on his face, he wasn't getting much sleep.

He set five packages of diapers down on the belt, and I decided to help him. I scanned one package and then pretended to scan the rest. I knew it was stealing, and today I'm not proud of it, but I felt like I had done my good deed for the day and that it helped him in some small way.

Little did I know that I'd be in his shoes a year or two later, selling extra cans of baby formula on eBay to help pay the bills.

Despite the lousy paycheck, I kept working at the store because it got me out of the house, which felt dead and airless.

I didn't want to be around my father. But the small acts of rebellion I'd committed while living at my mother's house were nothing compared to my next project.

When I was in high school, a friend made me a fake ID. I never was much of a drinker, but I thought it would be cool to have one. After all, it's a victimless crime, so what's the big deal? Yeah, I'm a couple years younger, but you can go off to war and not be old enough to drink. That was my justification.

At the time, the internet was just getting started. There was AOL and CompuServe, and eBay was starting to become popular. There was no such thing as high-speed internet. Dial-up service was the norm, so it was really slow.

In addition to searching for cheap Nautica T-shirts online, I had discovered the world of online pornography.

Before I lose you completely, stay with me here.

I found a company that offered a subscription service with five or six new videos each month, like the Book of the Month club.

I signed up and downloaded the videos and thought my friends might want a copy too, so I burned a few DVDs for them. Word spread, and soon other kids at school were asking for videos, and how much did I want for them? Not surprisingly, I soon became the most popular kid in school, at least among the guys. The money started to roll in. Whenever another series of videos came out, I made more copies. I bought a multi-DVD burner so I could burn five DVDs at a time.

One day, I stumbled upon the adult section of eBay. It was pretty well hidden at the time, but I discovered thousands of DVDs I didn't know about, so I made more copies of the subscription videos and listed them for sale on eBay. I spent the summer burning videos and going to the post office, pulling in almost $1,000 each week.

It never occurred to me that the videos were copyrighted material. After all, if it was illegal, then I shouldn't be able to copy DVDs, right? Besides, just like with my fake ID, I didn't think I was hurting anyone, so it was okay.

I used photos from the subscription website as the images for my auctions, so I was essentially tricking people into thinking that they were getting an original video instead of a bootleg DVD in a jewel case. I justified it because I was charging a fraction of the original cost, and besides, I was providing a service to the world. I was your local filth merchant.

You're welcome, everyone. If you want cheap porn, gimme a call.

I eventually discovered that someone was selling the same videos that I was selling, so I bought one of his DVDs and found that it was an exact copy of one of *my* DVDs. Someone was ripping me off? I couldn't believe it. Who steals from Robin Hood? The audacity! Then again, I was ripping off the subscription service, so I didn't say anything and just kept cashing the checks.

A few weeks later, the guy who was selling copies of my copies sent me a message. He told me that the subscription service had sent him a cease and desist letter and ordered him to shut down his business. At first I thought he just wanted to squeeze me out, so I waited to see if he kept selling them. When his account was terminated about a week later, the writing was on the wall: it was time for me to stop too. I closed my account and got rid of my DVD burner.

Today, I'm not proud of the fact that I did something so blatantly illegal, but it clearly sparked something in me. I loved everything about running my own business: from dealing with customers to filling orders and making money, lots of it. I was my own boss, and no one was telling me what to do.

It also proved that there's money to be made out there if you offer a service that's not convenient or readily accessible, and one that people really want. Selling pirated porn DVDs taught me about the service industry as well as about supply and demand. Granted, it wasn't the most wholesome business out there, but the lessons I learned stuck in my head, and I filed them away for the future.

With my ill-gotten gains, I bought a used Dodge Neon, my first real car. I paid only a couple thousand dollars for it.

As was the case with the VCR and my mother's Geo Prizm, I wanted to understand how the car worked so I could fix it when something went wrong. I went online and looked for information on forums and websites. YouTube didn't exist yet, so I really had to dig for information.

The stereo in the Neon was pretty crappy, so I bought a new one and an instruction manual. I pulled out the old unit and installed the new one, and I was so proud of myself when I finished. Next, I installed the speakers, ran wiring for a subwoofer and then an air intake, and from there I just kept leveling up. Nothing broke, and I taught myself how to fix a car through trial and error. It made me feel alive.

I had discovered another way to feel alive: I started dating a girl named Jackie, my very first girlfriend. Every minute that I wasn't working on the car or in school, I was spending time with her. She made me feel valued, like I mattered to someone. Plus, it was another way to avoid my father. I wanted to chase girls, not help him pick out stuff at Building #19.

But I couldn't totally avoid him. It was my senior year of high school. I'd found my niche working on cars, and I wanted to become an auto mechanic after I graduated, but my father insisted I go to a four-year college instead and major in computer science.

We had a huge falling-out because he couldn't understand why I loved cars so much. The standoff lasted several weeks, which bumped up against deadlines for college applications. But my father wouldn't budge. He told me that fixing cars was not going to pay the bills and that I had to do what made sense.

He finally told me that he would pay a portion of my college tuition, but if I chose not to go then I'd be on my own. He wore me down, and I started to believe that I would be a failure if I didn't go to college and that people would look down on me. In high school, the very first question people ask when you're close to graduation is "What school are you going to?" Depending on the answer, they will either welcome you with open arms or look at you like you just touched their no-no square. "Hey look, there goes the kid who isn't going to college." Besides, that's where everyone else was headed, straight to college.

So I gave in and applied to UMass Boston, UMass Amherst, Suffolk University, and Harvard. I was shocked when I was accepted into the computer science department at Harvard. I really wanted to go to Suffolk because it seemed like a far more down-to-earth school—and cheaper—but it felt like I shouldn't pass up the opportunity to go to an Ivy League school, so I accepted.

I mean, who wouldn't?

PACK RAT

Hi, my name is Rich, and I'm a hoarder.

Hi, Rich!

I'm also a lifelong car nut, and anyone who works on cars for any amount of time is all about holding on to things they might need at some point in the future. I will typically keep a part to the point where I really need to give it away, sell it, or recycle it for scrap. I use plastic takeout containers to organize screws, nuts, and bolts and to store my tools. I reuse Amazon boxes to ship my own stuff.

Maybe I'm driven by my cheapness, but I always find a way to recycle something. Even today, I still buy used clothes. Why not? Most people buy a used house, even though they know that toilet has been used thousands of times already. But you clean it and move on, right? Why not sweatshirts as well? I can't stand to throw something away when it still serves a purpose.

I come at this honestly: My mom and dad are both world-class hoarders because they didn't have much when they were growing up. They came to America and made a life for themselves, but they never let go of their Caribbean mindset to save everything because they never knew what was looming just over the horizon.

The dark flip side to hoarding is that I'm impulsive and absent-minded. When I get frustrated working on a car and can't find the right tool, I'll go out and buy a new one instead of taking the time to look for it—the one instance where my impulsivity overrides my cheapness. At the end of the day, I'll have seven of the same tool but can't find any of them.

My youngest daughter loves to collect trash and make something new from it. She'll pick up a paper clip on the ground and use it in an art project. She also loves to experiment and find out how things work. One day she put some blueberries in a glass of water and said she wanted to make blueberry juice because blueberry juice is very expensive. Apparently, at least with her, the apple—or berry—doesn't fall far from the tree.

MY BEST BRO

My brother Roderick is ten years older than me. We don't share the same father, and we didn't spend a lot of time with each other while growing up. My mother left Trinidad to go to Puerto Rico to have my brother so he could have US citizenship, and then she brought him back to Trinidad to be raised by his grandparents while she moved to the United States so she could get a better footing in America and provide a better life for her family.

I always chuckle when I tell people I have a Puerto Rican brother. It makes me sound like Mr. Worldwide.

Different dads meant different upbringings and cultural backgrounds, and since he was so much older than me, we didn't have much in common and we didn't always get along.

But I loved my big brother, and I thought he was the coolest guy in the world. I loved to listen to his Ice Cube, Eric B. & Rakim, and Public Enemy tapes and records, and he is the foundation for the music that I still listen to today. After he joined the Marines, we lost touch for a while, but we reconnected and now we talk and text frequently.

He's my number one fan.

CHAPTER THREE

ESCAPING THE BARREL

From day one at Harvard, I never felt completely comfortable. Most of the students came from money, and most of them were well-spoken and had more prominent backgrounds than me. I could put on a facade to some extent, but I couldn't pretend that I was someone else.

I was also surrounded by people who didn't look like me. In fact, when I received my acceptance letter from Harvard, I was actually a bit insulted that they took me. Did they only accept me because I'm Black and they had to fulfill a certain quota? Am I really that smart? I knew I was smart but not *that* smart. How did I really get in here? I felt intimidated, and even today I still think about it.

Plus, freshman year was one big popularity contest. Everyone was fresh out of high school, so the teenage mentality still prevailed, only it was on a higher social and income level than I was used to. There was a lot of *What do you have?* and *Who do you know?* and *Who are your parents?*

Then there were the teachers. Maybe it was because I was majoring in a subject that I wasn't passionate about, but the teachers really rankled me. Years later I would marry a teacher, and I've always been fascinated and curious about the psychology behind teachers in general. At the time, I looked at them and thought, *Why do I have to listen to this guy? He's reading out loud from a book that someone else wrote, and then he's going to quiz us about what's in that book. Why can't I just read the book myself?* Even though it was Harvard, the rebel in me mostly found the classes there to be a waste of time.

Maybe I should have spent more time studying, because when I found out that Jackie was pregnant, my free time would become virtually nonexistent.

Maybe I should have spent more time with my dad at Building #19.

My father was livid.

We'd had our struggles of course, but he considered this to be my greatest betrayal because I had done something that he'd spent his life warning me about. He had told me time and again that people were going to assume certain things about me because of my skin color. In his view, getting a girl pregnant while I was still a teenager was just confirming the world's assumptions that that's all I was good for.

I had never agreed with my father about much, and I wasn't about to start now, so we decided to have the baby and get married. I wanted to make sure I was doing the right thing, and we'd figure things out as we went.

I don't have to say that we were both very young, and very naive.

When my daughter Breanna was born, I got a job working the graveyard shift at a hotel on the weekends and continued going to classes, but it was anything but easy.

I moved into Jackie's house, where I lived with five other people: Jackie—who had a full-time job as a medical biller—my daughter, my mother-in-law, Jackie's brother, and her special-needs cousin. I think there were also six or seven cats. The chaos of the household brought me back to growing up with my mother and my aunts, but my life was radically different from that earlier time. After I came home from school and work, I didn't leisurely tinker with stuff before the others arrived. Instead, now I was usually the last one home at night. I'd grab a quick meal before spending a few minutes with my wife and daughter and hitting the books for a few hours. I'd manage a few hours of sleep before waking up and starting all over again.

We were on food stamps and WIC, and we barely had enough money to cover our bills, but I never asked my parents for help. Restarting my business selling pirated porn DVDs wasn't in the cards, but was there anything else I could sell on the web? I had a few extra parts that I had stockpiled for the Neon, so I put them up for sale. Once they sold, I looked around for other stuff I didn't need anymore.

When Breanna started eating solid food, there were a few extra cans of baby formula from WIC just sitting around. It was selling for sixty bucks a can, which was crazy money to us back then, so I listed and quickly sold the excess online.

With a little extra money in my pocket, I could breathe a bit easier, so I continued to look around for more stuff to sell to help make ends meet.

Back then, most towns had electronic repair shops that would fix broken TVs, radios, and other household appliances. If you looked in the back room of such a shop, you'd see huge piles of steel cases, cables, TV tubes, and other electronic detritus. The appliances no longer worked, but their parts could extend the life of a broken VCR or record player.

Since my family was filled with hoarders and scavengers, we had a huge stockpile of broken electronics. I checked and, sure enough, lots of people were already selling their old parts online.

I sprang into action, listing and selling my broken electronics, everything from old cameras to MP3 players, which helped relieve some of the financial strain.

Even though I was still mad at my father, I fully realized that by selling my old junk I was honoring his hoarding ethos. After all, there's no good reason to throw something out when there's still a little life left in it. To this day, I still have all—far too many—of the broken and outdated electronic devices I've owned through the years: all my cameras, cell phones, Discmans, Walkmans, everything. You just never know when you'll need them.

If there's still some meat on that bone, don't throw it away.

I lasted two years at Harvard.

When I transferred to Suffolk University for my junior year, I had definitely found my people. Suffolk was more diverse than Harvard, and most of the students fell into my economic demographic. Many lived in the inner city, commuted to campus, and held down at least one outside job, typically two or three. I never saw anyone get picked up in a Mercedes; in fact, a lot of them didn't even have cars.

I settled into life at Suffolk. In addition to carrying a full course load, I worked in the computer lab helping students with programming and projects.

Today, I think that going to Suffolk brought out my hustler spirit, because I really had no choice but to hustle. I had to work; I had to make money. Lather, rinse, repeat. But there was little time for anything else. I felt trapped and frustrated. Something had to give.

Turned out it was my marriage, which didn't even last a year. It didn't work out because we were young—too young—and we both still wanted to explore the world around us.

The divorce was straightforward. We didn't own a house, so the judge just cut our credit card debt in half to settle things. I spent every other weekend with Breanna, but I also had to pay $600 a month in child support. It seemed high since I was only making $30,000 a year at the time, but I chalked it up to *It is what it is*. I was young and broke, with an ex-wife and a baby.

I finally got that this was what my father had been talking about.

I moved in with a roommate and got on with my life. It was sometimes difficult to continue when it seemed like half the world was out going to bars and partying, and I had to work the night shift and then take Breanna to swim lessons in the morning.

At the time, I didn't have much. The Neon wasn't a great car and it was pretty bare-bones, but it was cheap and I learned the basics of how cars worked.

I graduated from Suffolk in 2004 with a degree in computer science and a minor in mathematics. I got my first real job as the IT help-desk guy at a publishing company in Burlington, Massachusetts.

What does a car guy do when he gets his first real job? He buys his first real car!

As soon as I could afford it, I upgraded to a Neon SRT-4, the souped-up version of the bare-bones Neon, and I couldn't wait to get started. There was so much I could do to increase the power, and I did it all in fits and starts. I upgraded the exhaust, the wheels, and the intake and installed a bigger turbocharger. I was the only guy at work with a modified car. It wasn't much compared to the Mercedes and Lexus everyone else drove, but it was mine and it was fast.

At work, I spent most of my time crawling under desks and asking, "Have you tried rebooting your computer?" Within a few years, I moved to an investment banking company and was promoted to system administrator, where my primary job mostly consisted of fixing networking and server issues and my secondary job was again asking people if they had tried rebooting their computers.

When I worked in the financial district, my attire changed completely. Suddenly I was big into fashion and looking good, because everyone around me had to look good and dress professionally for their jobs. They had an image to maintain. Plus, now I had a little money to spend. I wore a good pair of slacks, a dress shirt, a tie, and nice shoes. I enjoyed dressing up for work and felt like it helped me to fit in, just like in high school. I learned all the high-end fashion brands and that you never wear a black belt with brown shoes, though sometimes I forgot this.

The executives at work made me look at how I presented myself. I wanted to elevate myself to their level. You know, show me the five people you hang out with and I'll show you who you are.

I loved my coworkers—most of them—but I wasn't thrilled about working a full-time job. In every single photo I have of my dad, his face just screams disappointment. He absolutely hated working for someone else, and ever since I was a kid, he talked about how anyone who works for someone else is stuck in a rat race with little chance of escaping, though he liked to describe it as crabs in a barrel.

All the crabs are trying to climb out of the barrel, but they have to step on another crab in order to get a little higher. Finally, if one crab starts to make it out, then the other crabs use his legs as leverage to pull themselves up and out. The tragedy is that the fewer crabs there are in the barrel, the less chance that the others have of climbing out because they have to step on one another to get up.

Once I had been working full-time for a few years, I finally understood what he was talking about. Whenever I complained to him about my job, he teased me that I was just another crab in a barrel. But when I reminded him that he told me that a college degree was supposed to prevent all this, he laughed and said that a Black man needs his papers to show that he's educated and that I needed them to enter into the professional workforce. From there, where I went was up to me.

I felt trapped and didn't understand what I was supposed to do. My true passion was cars: being around them, thinking about them, and talking about them. When I was working on mine, I didn't have to answer to anyone. Plus, my cars gave me so much joy compared to restarting computers and resetting employees' usernames and passwords. I also liked selling stuff online because the end result was determined by the effort I put into it. When it comes to most jobs, people know exactly what they can get away with. They can do or say certain things, and at the end of the day they're still going to get paid. But working for yourself, it's *Insert coin to continue*. You want to make money? Fine, but you have to do something. You have to push the button to get the bacon.

The harder I worked, the more money I made. Fast-forward to today: if I take some time off and don't release a video, I don't get paid.

It's a lot tougher, but I definitely prefer the hustle to the barrel of crabs.

In addition to selling broken electronics and baby formula online, I started to buy stuff locally to resell. When the iPhone first came out in 2007, you could walk into an Apple Store and buy one for around $250 without signing up for a plan. Since Apple Stores only received a limited supply of iPhones, people who lived in iPhone deserts bought them online, and they were willing to pay a lot more than the retail price.

There were more than enough iPhones to go around at my local store, so I took a chance and bought two. I kept one and immediately sold the other online for $450.

The next day, I started buying up as many iPhones as I could find. The limit was five per person, but I brought a friend with me so I could buy ten, and I sold them all online in a few days. Back then, YouTube was still relatively new, and since there weren't that many videos to choose from it didn't take much for a video to go viral. I was making so much money from reselling iPhones that I made a video where I dropped a brand-new iPhone in a glass of water and ran a timer to see how long it took for the phone to fail. That was my first real video.

I also started buying salvaged and wrecked Dodge Chargers to take apart so I could sell the parts online, and I joined those forums to advertise the parts I was selling.

In fact, I was so active buying and selling things online that I almost didn't have time for my regular job.

One day at work, I was helping an executive with his computer. At the time, I was researching luxury watches, and I noticed he was wearing a Panerai, a higher-end luxury watch brand. He frequently fidgeted with the watch, checking the time every few minutes and playing with the strap.

I knew I wanted one, but exactly *why* I wanted one, I wasn't sure. If millionaires owned that type of watch, then I felt I needed one to become successful. This was odd, and very backward, because, after all, it takes lots of money to appear rich to total strangers.

"Nice watch," I said one day.

"Do you know what this is?"

He sounded a bit defensive. At the same time, I was offended that he assumed that I didn't know anything about high-end watches. I mean, after all, I was just the IT guy, *of course* I knew about luxury wristwatches! So I started rattling off everything I knew about the manufacturer, from the history of the brand to the specifics of that very watch.

I like to think that, after I finished my Hamlet-style monologue, I earned a tiny bit of respect from him. Whenever I worked on his computer after that, we talked about watches.

I decided that when I made it, I would buy that same watch. In the meantime, I met the woman who would become my second wife, though things got off to a rocky start—not between us, but with her family.

Trust is huge in my book. Once I decide to do something, it's as good as done. Time and time again, I've proved that I can do whatever I set my mind to. And if anyone doubts that I'll be able to accomplish something, then I really don't want them on my side.

When I met Allison's parents, I had three strikes against me.

Strike one: I was Black, and their daughter was white. (I can hear my dad's voice already.) In the mid-2000s, Black people weren't that common in Salem, Massachusetts—yes, the Witch City—and neither were interracial relationships.

Strike two: I was bringing baggage into the relationship because I was divorced and raising a child with another woman.

Strike three: I wanted to buy a run-down three-family apartment building in a rough neighborhood with their daughter. Not only were we not married but I was asking her to supply the down payment because at the time I didn't have much money to spare. Plus, we were going to live in one of the units.

Okay . . . twelve strikes.

The four of us were standing in front of the building I wanted to buy, which was located on a busy street across from a liquor store. I remember her parents' faces like it was yesterday: a mixture of shock and horror. They looked at me like I was a chimney sweep.

I explained my plan to them just as I had explained it to Allison, who was fully on board with me.

"We're going to buy a house together so we can set ourselves up for the future. We'll live in one unit and rent out the others, which will cover the mortgage. We'll save up enough money to buy another building and rent it out, then we'll buy a very nice house, and Allison will be able to drive whatever car she wants, and so will I. We'll make a few sacrifices now, and in a few years it's going to pay off."

Her parents had their doubts, but to their credit, my future in-laws decided to trust me.

In the end, everything turned out exactly how I'd predicted. We bought that building and then another one, fixed them up, and rented them out. Then we bought a brand-new house—no used toilets—in a quiet neighborhood and gave Allison's parents two grandkids.

If you're reading this, you're welcome.

Becoming a father when I was basically a kid myself had emboldened me. After all, I'd already proved I could do something with the odds stacked against me. I could go to school, I could have a kid, and I could work. And I could still have cool stuff.

In fact, that's become my life theme: You think I can't do that? Just watch. I'm going to prove you wrong.

But even I had to admit that the first time I sat in the front seat of Dolores, ready for her maiden voyage, I had my doubts.

Very big ones.

MAN UP

In this day and age, being what's called a man is certainly bittersweet, because when it comes to showing emotions, we're damned if we do and damned if we don't. I think society in general just teaches men to shut up and figure, *It is what it is*. And if you're a young boy, your dad may have said to you at one point—or will probably say—"What are you crying for? Only girls cry. Suck it up. And man up."

Not too long ago, I was visiting a friend who was going through a divorce and I asked him how he felt. Once he started talking, it was like a dam burst and he couldn't stop. At one point, he said he never got the chance to talk about what he was going through, not only because he thought that it would alienate his friends and parents, but also because they assumed he was keeping a stiff upper lip about the whole situation, like most men.

After all, we usually don't talk about this kind of stuff with our friends—with anyone, actually. We're soldiers. That's how we're socialized. We're taught to not express emotion. Wait, are you crying? Are you a *girl*?

Not only do most men view showing emotion as weakness, but in many cases women hate it too. Whenever I've cried in front of a woman, I didn't get the reaction or comfort I thought I would. Instead, she told me that *I* was expected to be the strong one and if anyone was crying it should be her.

I believe the actual words were "You're my rock."

The not-so-hidden message: *Maybe I need to find a more masculine guy.*

Since then I've gone back to crying in cars. At least they don't judge me.

I get it. I have three kids and a wife, and I'd do anything to provide for them. Men want to be viewed as the protectors and providers for their families, and that's been ingrained in us—male, female, and other—for thousands of years. Just a couple of tears, the slightest moment of weakness, can undo everything. But if someone is hurt—physically or emotionally—and needs help, you help them. That's what people do, and that's also ingrained in us. You don't freeze and ask, "Why are you crying?"

I know how I would want to be treated if I was going through a situation like that. My friend felt very lonely until I listened to him, *really* listened to him, a skill that's in increasingly short supply these days.

And I am raising my son Henry differently.

————————————————————————

————

————————————————————————

LOSING MY RELIGION

When I was a kid, I believed in God. I went to Catholic school, and religion was part of my daily life: wake up in the morning, brush your teeth, say your prayers. When you have Caribbean parents, well, there isn't much choice.

Every day, it was drilled into me that there's a God up there and I had to make him happy by whispering to him at night, because if I didn't, I'd go to hell. Secretly, I thought this sounded a bit harsh, but I obviously didn't want to go there, so I tried to behave. I prayed every single night. My father was very religious and he always told me to pray, because if I didn't, God would get mad. God loves you, but if you sin and don't ask for forgiveness, you will be condemned to eternal punishment in hell. So guess what I did every night?

When I graduated from college, all my friends were getting cars and vacations and expensive presents. My father gave me a Bible. He also gave me one for my high school graduation. That was his way of connecting with me, and also of sending a message. I started reading the Bible more, and I thought, *Wow, these stories are insanely difficult to follow, but it seems that at least God has a sense of humor.*

One of my faves was Job, a God-fearing man who never did anything wrong. One day, God and Satan made a bet that if God took everything away from Job that he would curse God. So God slaughtered his ten kids, livestock, and servants. He also gave him skin lesions. Most of Job's friends told him that God wasn't very nice, but Job never cursed God despite all his hardships. Satan lost the bet, and God gave Job back his health, more property, and ten *new* kids, which I thought was a pretty odd way to prove a point. But even then, where did the new kids come from? I'd think he would still want his old kids back, right? I mean, they aren't cattle.

One day, I forgot to pray. I was just too tired. The next day, I suddenly remembered that I had forgotten to pray.

Surprisingly, I didn't drop dead. Since I'm very analytical, I decided to run an experiment: I wouldn't pray for a week just to see what would happen. The hypothesis: Do bad things happen to you when you don't pray?

After a week, nothing happened. I lived normally with the usual ups and downs, same as when I'd prayed before. The following week, I prayed every day and still had the normal ups and downs. There was no discernible difference, so then I really stopped praying.

For several years, I was also a bit obsessed with doing things three times: if I tapped a door three times before leaving a room, or tapped a glass of water three times before drinking it, it meant that I'd have a good day and that no one would die.

After I stopped praying and nothing bad happened, I questioned whether tapping something three times had any effect. The first time I decided to not tap my glass and just drink the water, lo and behold, nothing happened. So the tapping disappeared as well, and that was over twenty-five years ago.

CHAPTER FOUR

GAINING TRACTION

Very early on, when I first started working on cars, I got into the habit of tightening screws with my fingers. After all, I didn't have the money to buy the proper tools and did the best with what I already had.

Later on, when I could afford power tools and specialized wrenches, I still preferred using my hands instead of a wrench or tool, because as the car got closer to being done, I was super excited about getting it out on the road, and sometimes I didn't take extra care to really tighten things down.

Don't get me wrong, the nuts aren't going anywhere, at least not for the first couple of miles. The times when I've tested them later with a power drill, I find that they're usually pretty tight.

But I will admit that the hand-tight philosophy has spilled over into other parts of my life, because I get bored very quickly and get really excited to move on to the next thing. Once I've accomplished enough of what I think is necessary for me to consider a project successful, I'm ready to move on to the next one. Okay, I've proved that I can do this, so now it's time to do the next thing so I can prove myself all over again.

After countless false starts and scraped and bloody knuckles— not to mention more than a few bone-rattling electrical shocks—Dolores was finally ready to take out on the road, a full year after she landed in my driveway, inoperable and reeking of rotting fish.

As I steered the car out of the garage, crazy things ran through my head. I'd spent thousands of hours and tens of thousands of dollars over the last year to bring her back to life. What if she died halfway down the block? What if my father was right, and working on cars was stupid? Maybe I should have stayed in my lane.

But I knew that even if Dolores didn't make it more than a block, she—and I—would still be a success. It would be a massive, albeit expensive, learning experience.

I sat frozen in the driver's seat while all this rolled through my head. Again it would be Before Tesla and After Tesla, only this time on a completely different level.

I held my breath and gingerly stepped on the accelerator.

While I was working on Dolores, whenever I wanted to give up, I'd just take some time off, because back then there was no rush. I was in my early days of making videos, and competition for eyeballs wasn't so cutthroat. In fact, I'm not sure if the term "influencer" was even around. It was more like, *Hey, I just released a new video on Dolores, and in another two months I'll release another video on Dolores.*

Today, the competition is just brutal. I have to frequently come up with new videos because if I don't, I quickly become irrelevant, which means the algorithm no longer promotes my videos. When your videos don't get promoted, nobody watches them, and when nobody watches them you don't get paid, and when you don't get paid you have to sell your house.

Fixing Dolores was like fitting pieces of a puzzle together, especially once I had the two cars side by side in my garage. As I moved parts from Slim Shady to Dolores over and over again, I learned firsthand how the cars were put together. For example, when I removed the driver's seat from Slim Shady, I knew exactly how to install it in Dolores.

Trying to fix a VCR when you're a child is one thing. When it came to Dolores, the goal was always to end up with a car that ran and drove, which was never guaranteed.

What if Dolores failed? That question was never far from my mind, especially because, by then, hundreds of thousands of people were following along on YouTube. And we were *all* in the dark. Was this plane going to crash? I didn't know, but I wanted to watch.

One reason my channel had become so popular was because electric-car technology was so new back then, and no one knew anything about it. I was trying to teach viewers about it on my channel while also learning about it myself.

But what *if* Dolores failed? Other people may have viewed me as a failure—and indeed, perhaps more than a few were rooting for me to fail—but I wouldn't have regarded it as a personal failure. In the end, everybody else and I would have learned something, whether she ran or not.

Just like with the VCR.

I'll never be able to put into words how I felt at that very moment when the car lurched forward. The first few moments that I drove Dolores were such an out-of-body experience that I blanked out. It was as if I had actually *become* the car; there was absolutely nothing separating us.

I *was* Dolores.

I steered the car onto the street and was completely overwhelmed. I think I cried, but I honestly don't remember. I had taken two cars that had both been given up for dead and created one beautiful car that was now racing down the road. I'd thought I could do it—I had *dreamed* of doing it—but now I had proof that every decision I had made over the past year was the right one.

When Chad had shown up in my driveway with the first Tesla I'd ever seen, it was an amazing experience because I'd never driven a car like that before. I thought it must be what it would be like to drive twenty years in the future.

But Dolores was completely different. After all, it wasn't something that a bunch of engineers did. The only reason she ran was due to my hard work.

Word spread about Dolores, and podcasts and blogs devoted to Teslas and other electric vehicles, as well as mainstream news outlets, contacted me for interviews.

Somewhere along the line, a reporter referred to me as the Dr. Frankenstein of Teslas. It's a snappy sound bite, but I wasn't crazy about the term. For one, calling me the doctor of anything makes me feel weird. I've always considered myself to be a shade-tree mechanic. I'm not professionally trained and I didn't go to school to learn how to fix cars, so I've always kind of had a problem with being called an expert in anything... well, except sarcasm. Besides, I was mostly just playing around with Dolores, even though I hoped that all my hard work would eventually bear fruit. After all, Dr. Frankenstein had a clear mission from day one, while I was essentially just twisting wires together and hoping for the best.

With so many new viewers, I felt obligated to improve the videos, but as more people read about me and tuned into the channel, the number of trolls increased exponentially. A comment like "I didn't know Black people could work on cars. I thought they just stole stuff" was one of the tamer examples.

Online, everyone's hiding behind a mask. They're anonymous. And when you hide behind a mask, you're able to show your true colors and do and say whatever you want because people have no idea who you are. I was still posting my videos on the Tesla forums in addition to scanning other posts—because I sometimes got ideas for videos from reading what others were posting and commenting on—but the negative comments were starting to wear on me. I was so new to all this video stuff and I didn't understand. I'd seen plenty of trolls on forums, but this time they were all talking about *me*! There weren't many, and I could usually breeze through a whole bunch of comments in twenty minutes, but it was difficult to resist reading messages that some people posted because they specifically wanted to hurt me.

You can come across as dead on the inside as much as you want, but after a certain amount of time the trolls will start to affect you, because we're all people and we all want some sort of approval. This is especially true online, since leaving a comment is the only way that most viewers correspond with a creator or influencer. At the time, even though most of the comments were overwhelmingly positive, I felt that I was utterly alone and what I was doing was terrible.

My days took on a certain rhythm: wake up, brush my teeth, read comments.

One day, I'd had enough and decided to turn the lens on the people who were leaving the negative comments by pinning the most disgusting, racist posts to the very beginning of the section, which reduced them by about 80 percent. After being in the game for a while, I just chuckle now. Clowns can make fifty grand a year, and here these commenters were being ones for free.

But I was still stressed out. What was initially a hobby had morphed into a second full-time job. I bought a few more salvaged Teslas to scavenge for parts for myself and to sell to others. My garage and basement looked like an auto parts warehouse. The advertising revenue from YouTube was growing each month, but it didn't come close to matching my take-home pay.

Still, someone was actually paying me to take things apart and repurpose them. What a concept. I felt like a million bucks, but part of me doubted the whole thing, like, *There's no way this is real. Someone's playing a joke on me.* I just didn't think I would be worthy of this kind of attention. I kept thinking, *Who do I have to thank for this? There's no way I built this myself.* I felt that way for a long time.

Along with an increase in viewership and public profile, I had to deal with my first legal issue when I received a cease and desist letter from CarGurus.com, an online car sales website, about the name of my channel: *CarGuru.* In a way, I had been expecting it, so I had already started to brainstorm a new name. How about *Teslas with Rich?* It was pretty straightforward, and, after all, that was the focus of the channel at the time. But what if I stopped working on Teslas in the future? Everything was so new to me. Although I couldn't picture it, I knew that, given my short attention span, I also couldn't rule it out.

Okay, next. My name is Rich. What will I *always* be doing, whether it's cars or something else? No matter what it is—watches, stereos, VCRs—I'll want to take it apart, and then I'll want to rebuild it.

What about *Rich Rebuilds?*

It sounded good and the rhythm worked. Plus, it was broad enough to cover anything I'd want to tackle in the foreseeable future. At this point, Carl Hewitt, who had earlier said I should try my hand at videos, had come on board to help me edit them, and he thought the title worked. So we made the change.

If you look at the videos from my early YouTube days, you'll see that I dressed totally differently. Today my wardrobe mostly consists of sweatshirts and sweatpants and jeans, but back then when I worked on Dolores I wore dress shirts and slacks from my IT job. They were the only clothes I had, and I would never have dreamed of wearing a sweatshirt to the office. I gradually shifted to wearing more casual clothes on camera, since those dress shirts and slacks started to look disgusting after a week of slogging away in the garage. As a result, I ended up throwing away lots of clothes—well, recycling them, since I cut up my sweatshirts and used them as rags to clean cars. Remember? I *hate* throwing things away.

But the clothes were the least of it. To tell you the truth, I'm not all that comfortable being in front of the camera, and back then I was very stiff. I knew that I wanted to share my knowledge and progress on Dolores as well as on future cars, but it felt unnatural to have the camera pointed at me. Instead, I preferred to keep the lens on the part I was working on, because playing back the video during edits only magnified all my weird unconscious tics. It seemed like I was constantly touching my nose, rolling my eyes, and scratching something. Every single insecurity I thought I had buried since high school rose up pretty quickly. *Do I really look like that?*

And do I really want to be in the spotlight?

But I really believed in what I was doing and felt I owed it to my audience to keep going, teaching them new things at the same time that I was teaching myself. Besides, thanks to Dolores, I had grown so much, and I was determined to reveal more of my personality in the videos. I started to relax and even crack some jokes on camera.

At least the camera provided a buffer between me and my fans, or so I thought, because it didn't take long before people started to show up at my house. It also didn't take long for things to get a little weird, and a little scary.

With some, it was pretty innocent. A guy—it was always a guy—would knock on my door and say he was a big fan of the channel and could I come take a look at something on his car?

I'm a nice guy—some would say too nice—so I thanked him for watching the channel but said that this was my home and I don't work on anyone's cars but my own.

All good, he was sorry for bothering me. I deleted my home address from my YouTube page and replaced it with a post office box, which cut down on in-person encounters but led to some unnerving incidents.

In one video, I said that I'd always wanted a dog and was curious about the Great Dane breed. Not long after, I received a package with a jar that contained a stillborn puppy. In the accompanying note, this "fan" explained that his Great Dane had recently had nine puppies and that one was stillborn, so he thought that I'd like to have it as a gift. He included a few tips on how to preserve it by regularly topping off the jar with alcohol and wrote his name and return address on the package.

I thought about going to the police, but it was unclear for what. The guy specifically said that he regarded the puppy to be art, a form of taxidermy. And his note wasn't threatening, at least not outwardly.

I could have sent the puppy back, but in the end I considered it to be the equivalent of someone sending me a nude painting—not that anyone's done that yet; however, I *am* open to it. I do put my post office box out there, so it's feasible that anyone could send me anything. There was nothing I could really do, but it was a very creepy, very strange gift.

I knew that starting a YouTube channel wasn't for the faint of heart.

But then again, neither is starting a business.

ON THE ROAD AGAIN

Whenever I buy a new car (that runs), I like to pick it up myself instead of having it delivered. It can sometimes take days to get somewhere and travel can be a hassle, but I've come to prefer it.

On the road, there's nothing to really distract me, and I'm excited to see and visit new places. I also feel like I'm accomplishing a concrete task.

More importantly, when I'm out on the road it feels like I'm controlling time instead of the other way around. After all, having a frequent video deadline can be a relentless taskmaster, where the clock controls me, so when I'm away from home without all my responsibilities staring me in the face, I can relax a little because it feels like I'm in control.

It also provides me with some much needed downtime, which is a rare commodity in my life. At home, I rarely have time to myself. I'm always conscious of what my kids are doing, if they've eaten, or if they need me to drive them somewhere, so it feels good to be on the road by myself, where I can go at my own pace and be alone with my thoughts.

Besides, car transport companies aren't very gentle on cars, so I'd usually rather pick up a car myself . . . at least that's the excuse I sometimes give.

WHAT KEEPS ME AWAKE AT NIGHT

Everything.

Everything keeps me awake at night. Since I have serious ADHD, my mind is always going 1,000 miles per hour in every direction. All. The. Time. I do manage to sleep for an hour or two here and there, but then it's right back to 1,000 mph, where my brain is filled with everything from "I should answer that text" and "I have to pay this bill" to "When was the last time I showered?" and "How much did a Volkswagen Beetle cost in the 1980s?" All this blasts through my brain in just a few seconds while I'm driving four hours to pick up a boat that I'd decided to buy forty-five minutes earlier.

Did I also mention that I'm impulsive?

This is why I have two hundred unread texts, ninety-seven voicemails, and thousands of unread emails on my phone. My daughter has accepted the fact that this is who her father is and that she'll have to text me two or three times before she gets a response.

But for some bizarre reason, I don't have anxiety, and I never really worry about anything. My scatteredness is just bits and pieces of excitement and joy that keep me alive, and I love the world around me. I also love the people around me, though I'll admit that sometimes they're best from a distance.

I'm also very optimistic and like to problem-solve for other people, which usually goes something like this: "Your mom and dad got a divorce? Damn, but now you get two Christmases!"

Or: "You lost all your money in a hedge-fund Ponzi scheme? Sorry about that. Let me buy you a book about which berries in the forest are edible."

I never sleep; I'm too busy solving problems.

CHAPTER FIVE

THE LAND OF LOST TOYS

Even though my buddy Chad had essentially launched my YouTube career by introducing me to my first Tesla, since he still worked for the company he was contractually forbidden from providing me with any help, service, or parts.

However, he was doing some odd jobs on the side for other Tesla owners, and he'd occasionally help me out by sourcing parts, explaining how some of the systems worked, and by wrenching on Dolores every so often.

At one point, I needed a replacement twelve-volt accessory battery for Dolores, but I couldn't find one anywhere. Chad told me to come by the Tesla service center and he'd see what he could do, but I had to pretend that I didn't know him and vice versa. *Fine.* I set the battery onto the counter in front of Chris Salvo, Chad's coworker, and asked for a replacement.

As a company, Tesla knows a lot more about you and your car than you think, since they record a lot of information about the owners of every car they sell, as well as how the car's been used. For instance, Tesla knows the exact number of times that the driver's seat has been moved since the car was new. If a driver tends to adjust the seat a lot, this information can be used to aid in warranty service. This example just scratches the surface.

The company also knows the names, addresses, and other identifying features of everyone who's ever owned a specific vehicle. I needed that battery, so when Chris asked for my VIN, I knew better than to give him Dolores's number, which was listed as a salvage vehicle, so I looked up a car that was listed on eBay and gave him that VIN instead.

He glanced up from his monitor with a funny look on his face. "Okay, Mr. Chen, can you please confirm your address?"

Busted.

Chris was like a lukewarm off-brand soda on a hot day, toeing the Tesla company line. I didn't like him very much at the time, but when I ran into him six months later at an EV car show, we chatted for a bit and he apologized for how he'd treated me at Tesla. When he told me he was fired for complaining to higher-ups about parts shortages and management issues in the service department, my pettiness toward him disappeared. Chris was running a side business finding and selling parts for EVs, and even though he was a bit miffed at my attempt to put something over on him, he did help me source some parts. Soon he, Chad, and I started hanging out together to work on cars. In fact, they actually helped me in a few early videos: Chris brought the parts, I filmed the episodes, and Chad did the wrenching. I couldn't show their faces in the video because Chad still worked for Tesla at the time, so I just focused on Chad's hands and referred to them as Chad's biscuit grippers.

As the channel grew, more people asked if I could fix their cars, though thankfully no one showed up at my house. I told them that I wasn't authorized to work on someone else's car professionally, but they kept asking. One day, I mentioned this to Chris, adding that it sounded like maybe a garage devoted to fixing electric vehicles could make for a decent business. Based on his experience working at Tesla, he already knew how backed up the service department could get, so the three of us started brainstorming.

We started small. Chris's mom lived in Seabrook, New Hampshire, and had a two-car garage that wasn't being used much. The next time that someone asked me to fix their car, I referred them to Chris. Soon he was spending several nights a week and most of his weekends fixing cars, and Chad and I would help out when we could.

Soon there was more business than we could handle, and besides, we all had full-time jobs. We figured that we had some kind of superpower here, so why didn't we try to combine forces and start something more permanent?

With that, the Electrified Garage was born.

We started looking at property and got some contractor quotes for a thousand-square-foot garage that came in for about $100,000. I did a fundraiser and figured that, with three hundred thousand subscribers at the time, if just one out of three people gave a dollar we'd be in pretty good shape. We sold bobbleheads, T-shirts, butter knives—the tool I used to take apart Teslas—and condoms, a nod to my days pushing porn DVDs.

It turned into an exercise in futility. A lot of viewers told me that they'd fork over fifty or a hundred bucks, but they wanted to see a business plan first, which I found fascinating. If they were talking about $5,000 or $10,000, then maybe, but it wasn't an investment, since we had nothing to offer but trinkets at the time. It was pretty surprising and taught me a lot of things about business, mostly that people work hard for their money and don't easily part ways with it.

We generated about $11,000 from the fundraiser, a little far from our goal, but not all hope was lost. I had stashed away most of my YouTube revenue in a bank account, so in the end I just cut a check for the remaining costs of about $100,000. The garage started to take shape, and we actually came in under budget because several companies donated tire machines and other equipment as a form of sponsorship on the channel.

Once construction was finished, we rallied our friends to help out. We threw painting parties and swapped electrical work in exchange for mentions in a video or mechanical services.

Everything was on schedule. But first we had to deal with a disaster that could have easily shut the entire business down before it even opened.

I love when I mess up, because then I can figure out how to fix it. As I've already said, taking something apart so I can put it back together is just about my favorite thing in the world, and it's pretty much the only thing that calms me down. That said, every mechanic—both amateur and pro—has at least a few stories about their brushes with death or serious injury while they're working on a car: a jack stand collapses while they're underneath repairing a brake line, or a stray shard of metal flies toward an eye.

The grand opening of the first Electrified Garage was just weeks away when I bought a vintage Disney toy car for my youngest daughter. Now that Dolores was finished, I was looking for other electric vehicles to feature on the channel. I planned to electrify Mr. Toad's Wild Ride car with two Tesla batteries, and I figured it would add to the credibility of the Electrified Garage: we can work on Teslas, but we can also build some pretty cool stuff. I stored it at my friend Lee's garage and worked on it in my free time. After the build was done, we drove it around for a little while and took it to a local EV car show.

One day when I wasn't there, Lee wanted to make sure the batteries were charged fully for our next adventure. Unfortunately, the charger he used wasn't rated for lithium batteries, and soon they started exploding and Mr. Toad caught fire. The garage had security cameras, so the whole thing was recorded in all its glory. When the fire department showed up, one of the firefighters asked if there was live ammunition in the car because it sounded like gunshots going off.

The fire was extinguished, and local media covered the story, which didn't make me look particularly good. The timing couldn't have been worse, because that's just when we had solidified plans to open the Electrified Garage.

I had a choice to make. I could blame my friend Lee and say this was all his fault since I wasn't there at the time, or I could say nothing and hope that everything blew over by the time the Electrified Garage opened.

Or I could showcase the explosions in a video as a way to show the dangers of working with EVs and accept full responsibility for the fire. I knew if I released this video, it could jeopardize my credibility as well as the future success of the Electrified Garage.

What to do?

In the end, it was my vehicle and my responsibility. I took a deep breath and posted "My First Tesla Battery Fire" to the channel and braced for the fallout, which surprisingly never came. Our plans for the Electrified Garage proceeded on schedule, and viewers were still getting in touch to ask if I could repair their $100,000 Teslas.

It was a good lesson to learn about how people would react to a potentially damaging video—or not—but if someone wanted us to fix their vintage Disney car, I'd probably tell them to go somewhere else.

"My First Tesla Battery Fire" had premiered the previous week, so when someone knocked on my door and I saw an unfamiliar guy standing on the front step, I wasn't sure if I should open the door.

I almost didn't, but today I'm happy that I took a chance, because that guy would help provide the key to my future success.

I opened the door a crack. "Can I help you?"

"Hi, I'm Billy Baker, a reporter from the *Boston Globe*. I want to talk to you about the Tesla."

I'm not the most organized person in the world, and email is not my favorite way to correspond with people. Honestly, between my job, the channel, and planning for the garage, I had no time to spare. If I don't respond, some people send a few emails before giving up. But this guy was relentless. At least once a week, he'd email and ask for an interview.

Part of the reason I ignored him is because I thought I had my first stalker. "How did you get my address?"

He explained that most newsrooms subscribe to a database that allows reporters to locate anyone anywhere, no matter how off the grid they are. I had no idea something like this existed, and I still think it's borderline creepy, maybe even a bit over the line, but I decided to talk to him because I thought he'd stop bugging me. We did the interview right there, and I showed him Dolores and my garage. The story came out on the front page of the *Boston Globe* a week later.

A few friends called to say they'd seen the story and thought it was cool, but I thought nothing more of it. It was March

2019, and I had recently done interviews with CNBC, local radio station WBUR, and *Business Insider*, so to me the *Globe* piece was a great story but, in terms of boosting my subscriber count, I didn't expect it to do much.

But then the story spread. And when the dust settled, my life would never be the same again.

Joe Rogan, the infamous comedian and podcaster, spent his formative years in Newton, Massachusetts, a suburb of Boston, and he still followed the local newspapers even though he had moved away early in his career, first to New York and then to Los Angeles.

When he read Billy Baker's profile of me, I guess something resonated for him. He posted a link on Twitter and on his Instagram account. At the time, Rogan had millions of people following him on social media, with millions more downloading episodes of his podcast, *The Joe Rogan Experience*, every month. Admittedly, he is a polarizing figure, but the exposure increased my YouTube subscribers and resulted in a few more media interviews.

I've never been into politics. I don't read the paper and rarely listen to the news. Sometimes I feel like I'm America's worst citizen because I'm so removed from the news, but then I ask: *What is the purpose of awareness?* I feel that a lot of the news today only exists to make people live in fear of something that will probably never affect them. For instance, what's the purpose of finding out the death toll from an earthquake in Syria? I just never saw the reason for it.

Some of my friends are really hard-core into politics, and they tell me that I have to vote for this person or that person. But over time, I've come to realize that no matter who's in office, Democrat or Republican, my life doesn't really change much. You voted for Biden or Trump or Obama. Great, but I still have to work in the morning and bring my kids to school. I still have to make money, so I focus my energies on making sure that the things that I *do* have control over are all set.

A lot of my friends are proud that they went into a booth and pushed a button, the bare minimum, but whenever I ask what they do besides that, I get crickets. Do they write to their local congressperson to incite change? Crickets. What about going to rallies to help raise awareness of a cause they believe in?

Yes, crickets again... but boy do they love to yell at the TV.

While I do acknowledge the importance of voting in local elections that directly affect your community, I've also seen what politics can do to people: it divides them and makes them upset. There are people who aren't willing to marry another person or have a life with another person because of their political beliefs, and I think that's kind of ridiculous. What if she's cute?

And then Rogan invited me to come on his show.

When the email first arrived from one of his producers, I thought one of my friends was playing a joke on me. The most listened-to man in the world wants *me* on his show? No way. No one cares about what I'm doing. After all, most of the people who appear on his show are total A-listers, some of the most famous in the world. Occasionally he'll invite a few B- and C-list celebrities, but never an E- or F-lister like me.

I'm literally a nobody from Boston, just some kid who was too cheap to buy a Tesla.

But like Billy Baker from the *Globe*, he was persistent and emailed me a few more times, and then I was scheduled to appear on the show on May 1, 2019.

I was beyond excited. My everyday life felt very small in comparison. I was still slogging away at my IT job, and I needed to take some time off to fly to Los Angeles to do the show. I also wanted to visit a couple of other EV YouTubers who I'd become friendly with over the last couple of years, most notably Simone Giertz, who invited me to work on her Tesla electric pickup truck that she had made from a Tesla Model 3.

But I had no vacation days left, so I asked my boss to make an exception for me. After all, how could I say no to such a great opportunity?

Unfortunately, my boss reminded me that I had no extra time off and we were already short-staffed due to other employees' preplanned vacations. This put me at a crossroads: Do I take a huge chance and accept what could potentially be my biggest break to date? Or do I play it safe and keep working at a job that provides benefits and some stability, but that I could do in my sleep?

I had already rebuilt a Tesla. It was time to rebuild my life.

I had to pass it by my wife, of course. She had every right to tell me, "No! Are you crazy? You have a family to support!"

But just as she had demonstrated when I first bought Dolores and then Slim Shady, Allison trusted me 1,000 percent. She knew I could accomplish anything that I set my mind to and told me it was fine with her if I quit my job.

I married the right woman.

I quit my job and flew to LA.

A few minutes before we went live, I was sitting in the studio wearing these big clunky headphones a few feet away from one of the most listened-to broadcasters in the world, and I thought I was hallucinating. I was sitting in the same chair that Barack Obama and Kevin Hart had sat in. Even Elon Musk had appeared a few months before. They must pipe some illicit substance into the studio's ventilation system, because it felt like one big mirage.

After all, just getting into the inner sanctum required numerous checkpoints and ID verifications. It's no surprise that the studio had security to rival that for heads of state, since Rogan has rabid fans and detractors on both sides.

The studio was located in a big, glass office park in Los Angeles. There were no signs and nothing to indicate what was inside. As I walked up to the front lobby, I noticed that the entire facade consisted of one-way glass, just like a police interrogation room: people on the other side could see you, but you couldn't see them. It was crazy, but obviously he had to be protected at all costs.

I was escorted into an area that is best described as a demilitarized zone, a kind of purgatory between the outside and inside worlds. I was everywhere and nowhere at once. After one person announced that I had arrived, someone else brought me into yet another inner chamber. I waited there for a bit before being taken into the next section, and then someone called the man himself to tell him that I had arrived. He finally showed up after fifteen or twenty minutes, and we settled in to do the show.

Once the ON AIR light lit up, a jolt of energy passed through the studio and we were off and running. We talked about Tesla stuff for twenty minutes, maybe twenty-five, and I quickly discovered that Joe Rogan doesn't want to talk about cars for three hours, so we moved on to other topics for the rest of the show, which was great for me because after talking about the same Tesla stuff over and over again, it's not hard to hear the enthusiasm drain from my voice.

Some of my friends and YouTube colleagues asked why he'd invited me and not them, and their jealousy was palpable. After all, most if not all of them were much better mechanics than me, and some had more subscribers and had been around a lot longer than *Rich Rebuilds*. Honestly, I also questioned why I was invited. But somewhere in the first hour of the show, it hit me: I wasn't invited on Joe Rogan because I was able to fix a car. I was invited because I did something that others were too scared to do. I took a flooded electric car—a disaster waiting to happen—and with no training and basic hand tools, I somehow made it work. And love him or hate him, people noticed.

I gained one hundred thousand subscribers in the first month after the show aired, and requests from other media poured in. The *Verge*, *Autoweek*, and *InsideEVs* all ran stories on me and the channel, which sparked a snowball effect peculiar to YouTube. When your following increases, YouTube promotes your videos more, which brings more subscribers, rinse and repeat. My increased visibility attracted more sponsors to the channel as well.

Once I quit my job, I was so focused on creating content for the channel that I stopped asking myself what I really wanted to work on. I had bought a Smart car with the idea of converting it to electric because I thought it was something that my audience of mostly Tesla-heads would like. After working on it for a couple of days, I was already bored, and I had to admit that I never really liked the car to begin with.

But I kept going because I thought a video series on the project would rack up half a million views and help add tens of thousands of subscribers to the channel. So I started taking it apart and chronicling it with unedited video snippets. But my interest in the car continued to plummet at a staggering rate. I was merely going through the motions.

I forced myself to take the whole car apart, and as I scanned the parts strewn across my garage floor, I thought, *That's it. I don't want to do this anymore.* I sold off the spare parts and chalked it up to bad decision-making.

I never named the car, and I never did a video about it either. But I ran into a problem. While I was taking apart the car, I posted some teaser pictures on Instagram with comments like, "Hey, I have a Smart car and I'm going to do something awesome with it." To this day, viewers will occasionally ask for an update on the Smart car, and I am forced to admit that I never finished it. As a result, I've learned not to tell anyone what I'm working on for a month or two, just in case I need to sweep it under the rug. That way, I can pretend the whole thing never happened. It also confirmed that I should only work on projects because I *want* to do them, not because I think they'll bring in more views and subscribers.

My income got a boost, which was a welcome relief in the wake of quitting my job. But I also had to adjust to my new life, one without a paycheck but where I called all the shots. I was in foreign territory. Everybody I knew had worked a nine-to-five job for their entire lives, and some lived in constant fear of losing that buffer. After all, for most Americans, the greatest fear is not knowing where their next paycheck is coming from.

I counted myself in that group as well. Even though I was free from the crabs-in-a-barrel race, it was also terrifying. Most of my friends and family had their doubts. My mom kept asking if I was sure I wanted to do this. To this day, she still doesn't know if I make money from YouTube or not. Others thought I was crazy, that I was dreaming, and there was no way I could make money this way. Why couldn't I stick with what I had been doing, working a full-time job and doing my other stuff on the side? Was that really so bad?

No, not really, except after more than a decade of listening to someone else call the shots, I felt like I was drowning. Just like my father, I had dreamed of escaping the rat race—and the barrel of crabs—for years.

I had finally climbed out.

When I got back from LA, the first thing I did was buy a watch that I'd been eyeing for a long time: a square Bell & Ross. I bought it to remind myself of the fifteen years that I'd spent working for someone else, and also that I was able to escape. I figured if things didn't work out with YouTube, I could always sell it.

As I write this, it's on my wrist. We'll see what next week holds.

Once I became the boss of me, I realized that every single decision was mine to make. I didn't have to brush my teeth in the morning if I wasn't in the mood, and I didn't have to maintain my beard to appease the boss and fit the company dress code.

I became more *me*, if that makes sense, and it didn't take long for my outward appearance to more clearly reflect who I am. As an inveterate people pleaser, I was fine with wearing the nice slacks and dress shirts to go to the office, but once I was out on my own, the only person I had to please was me. And what made me happy was being comfortable, so on the days when I was shooting a video I grabbed whatever jeans and sweatshirt were clean and didn't smell too bad. After all, I would be working on cars—a few oil stains and gashes are expected.

As a result, I felt more comfortable with being myself on camera. I cracked more jokes, made more asides, and ended up just being more me.

Years later, I went out and I bought the same exact Panerai watch that the executive at the office had. The only difference was that I didn't need to set the time, because now I was the boss, so I didn't have to answer to anyone else's schedule but my own. To this day, none of my watches show the correct time.

INTO THE DEEP END

When I was little, one of my uncles drowned because he ran into the water to save someone, even though he didn't know how to swim. I didn't want that for my own children, so I brought all of them to the local YMCA for swim lessons when they were just toddlers, starting over eighteen years ago with my first.

Today they're like fish in the water, and I like watching them splash around. But I hate the fact that I couldn't save them if something happened, and it's always bugged me.

One day in 2018, just as the channel was starting to take off, I decided to take a few private swimming lessons.

Even though the lessons were private, the pool was Olympic size. And it was packed. Kids were jumping off the diving board, babies splashed around in the shallow end, and senior citizens were doing laps. There I was, in my swim trunks and goggles holding a couple of pool noodles, and my teacher was showing me how to jump in the pool and not drown.

I was terrified, mostly because I felt everyone was staring at me. I had to learn how to swim from one side of the pool to the other, and it was incredibly humbling. Sure, I have ten cars, but can I swim without floaties?

But I did it. And while today I don't often willingly enter a pool or lake, at least I know I could save somebody if they were in trouble. I also felt emboldened to take more risks with the channel.

After all, if I could learn to do something most six-year-olds could do, I could do anything.

Tell the children of the future of my heroism.

———

WHO WROTE THIS?

My thoughts are loud. Very, *very* loud. My mind is always wandering; I can't shut it off. As a result, it takes me hours to relax and fall asleep.

I was never really a fan of drugs or smoking, but one day I decided to try a marijuana brownie to see if that would help. Boy, did it ever. The world opened up to me, and the monkey mind that normally plagues me completely disappeared.

A brownie puts me into a state where nothing's that big of a deal. Usually not much is a big deal, but now it's *really* not a big deal.

Now, every couple of days when I'm feeling fidgety or have a lot on my mind, I take a quarter of a brownie and my mood morphs completely. I become calm without taking something apart, which has never happened before.

I'll sometimes take a couple of bites before I brainstorm ideas for new videos. I'm a lot looser, everything is funnier, and I'm much more creative. I'll write down some notes for upcoming episodes, and after the drug wears off I'll look at the ideas and think, *Who the hell wrote this shit?*

Weed really changed my life. Now I can sleep without thinking of the time I threw up on my desk in second grade.

CHAPTER SIX

HOW THE SAUSAGE GETS MADE

When I was a kid, I didn't eat a lot of fast food. My aunts made home-cooked meals, lots of curry and vegetables and meat. We ate a lot of something we called *buss up shot,* which is Trinidadian for "busted-up shirt" because that's what it looks like: chickpeas, rice, and goat meat, sometimes chicken, whatever's on hand, gets all rolled up into a flatbread and eaten.

In other words, kind of like sausage: a little of this, a handful of that, throw it all together, and somehow it all works out in the end.

I make my videos the same way. Most of the time when I and my merry band of hoodlums that includes mechanics, fabricators, and welders shoot a video, I know which car or other conveyance I want to feature but rarely know how it's going to end...or start, for that matter. But that's why it works, because I operate best under pressure, and lots of it. Once I have a general idea of what the video's going to be about, I make a list of the things that I want to include and maybe write down a joke or some weird factoid to help explain what we're going to do. Sometimes I remember, and sometimes I don't.

What it boils down to is that we pull things out of our asses all the time—in other words, *buss up shot*. And when I quit my job to work full-time on the channel, that didn't change.

I laugh when someone asks if I have flowcharts or storyboards for each video. The truth is, the flowchart is in my brain. It's no secret that I have ADHD and I'm all over the place all the time. I also tend to have more ideas than I know what to do with, so I never worry that I won't be able to come up with an idea for a video.

Though the camera angles may look pretty slick, we don't use any fancy equipment to shoot our videos. Instead, we use iPhones to record everything because we want to capture the moment as realistically as possible. After all, if something funny is happening and we need to set up the lighting and focus, then we're going to lose the moment. To make sure that we don't miss anything, everyone who happens to be in the garage for the shoot has their iPhone running so we always have footage from several different angles to choose from during the editing process.

Once we think we have enough video, we add photos, video snippets, and commentary, and I'll make some edits to make sure that the story has a beginning, middle, and end. Then I'll review it for continuity and add comic relief to boost the humor quotient before stitching everything together to make the final video.

Then I hand it off to Carl to check the audio levels and make sure that nothing's really messed up before it goes live on YouTube.

That said, we sometimes screw up, and given our freewheeling process I'm actually surprised there aren't more mistakes. Whenever we create a brand-new video from scratch, I'm constantly Monday-morning quarterbacking, thinking how I could have done things better. Sometimes I don't explain things clearly enough. I am always the first to admit when I don't have a clue what I'm doing and that I'm learning as I go, so when viewers leave a comment saying they're not sure about a particular fix, I like to leave a more detailed explanation in the Comments section. I wish I had more time to answer questions, but, after all, viewers tune in to see a new video each week, and if I spent all my time answering questions, I'd have no time to make new videos.

Speaking of time, we try to make each video look seamless, but that can be extremely difficult to accomplish. Most people don't realize that videos aren't shot in a straight line from start to finish, since there are too many moving parts. Appearances can be very deceiving. The truth is that even though every video typically runs between twenty and thirty minutes, each minute of video usually takes at least an hour of wrenching and brainstorming, both before and during the shoot. After all, watching me talk to myself while I pace back and forth for ten minutes doesn't make for enjoyable content. So if I figure out an issue within twenty seconds in a video, that's because it's been heavily edited.

As a result, viewers often say that I make everything look so easy that they think a particular project is quicker and easier than it really is. On the flip side, others accuse me of not showing intermediate steps or safety protocols. But if we did that, the video would put viewers to sleep. Besides, most people only watch 30 percent of any given video, so it's almost not worth my time or theirs.

I've developed *Rich Rebuilds* to provide entertainment, and indeed, many viewers who know nothing about cars—some don't even know how to drive—tune in solely because I provide them with an entertaining video. It's just like watching a sitcom. If you learn something along the way, that's great, but I'm totally okay if you don't.

And if we screw up, we *want* you to laugh at us, especially since we take a slightly different approach from our competitors.

You see, most automotive YouTube channels—most DIY channels of any kind, for that matter—only feature projects that succeed. Viewers never see the efforts that totally tank, or even those that just don't turn out perfectly. When Carl and I first started working together, we decided that we would be honest with viewers and show my successes as well as my failures. You already know that I don't care if I fail at something because it means that I'll get to take it apart and put it back together and learn something new in the process. But there's a beneficial side effect: failures tend to provide much richer mines for comedy gold than successes.

I think people are drawn to my videos because they're spontaneous and the humor is never forced. There's also a sincerity that's evident when very little is planned out in advance and when I have no idea what I'm doing. After all, watching a bunch of guys wrestle with a transmission or wiring harness while bantering back and forth is just like real life. The sad truth is that many people live very isolated lives today, with most of their attention focused on their phones and electronic devices. As a result, there are a lot of incredibly lonely people out there, and some of them watch the channel because they think of us as their friends, as people they'd like to hang out with in real life.

Maybe we're the only friends they have.

I get that. I totally do. After I moved out of my mother's house and in with my father, I was incredibly lonely, and this was years before the iPhone came along. In a way, the channel has allowed me to re-create the energy of my childhood home. After all, I am a person who embraces chaos. I loved chaos when I was a kid; I loved the rush and uncertainty and the pressure. It's in my bones.

This is another reason I don't plan my videos: I get to go on a new adventure each week, combined with the challenge of walking a tightrope.

I was born to do this.

YouTube pays me based on the number of views each video generates, but another way to pay the bills comes in the form of sponsorships, advertisements about products and services that a manufacturer pays to include in each video.

When I first started out, product placements in YouTube videos were often very clunky and pretty amateurish. In fact, they were sometimes painful to watch. I decided to take a different path by injecting paid promotions right into the storyline of each video. Before I take a company on as a sponsor, they need to agree to give me creative control of the ad. After all, they're hiring me to do a job that they can't do themselves, and because I want the promotions to be seamless, they need to fit in with the overall tenor of the channel and the particular episode. In exchange for giving me creative control, I will produce the best ad that I possibly can.

Sometimes we shoot video for the sponsor spot separately and wiggle it into the episode. Most of the time, a sponsor doesn't want to see the whole video in advance, just the part that mentions their product, which is great because we are often tinkering with the video minutes before it goes live.

We have several sponsors that have done so well over the years that they advertise regularly. It can sometimes be a challenge to create a new ad for the same product several weeks in a row, but since our aim is to help them attract new customers, I try to brainstorm new bits each time. However, research claims that people have to see an ad a minimum of seven times before they make a purchase, so I guess it all depends.

Early in 2020, a company wanted to advertise their personal grooming tool to allow men to shave their genitals. It seemed a bit risqué, but since most of my viewers are men, I agreed, and of course I decided to have a bit of fun with it. The ad was slotted into the video "How Tesla Rewarded Me for Telling the Truth." I thought it would do well, since any video where I aim a few barbs at Elon and his company always attracts attention and a lot of viewers. The ad started at the 6:30 mark, when I turned my back and pretended to use the tool while sitting in my Tesla. This was followed by a demonstration of how to use the accompanying lotion and deodorant with a basketball that just happened to be handy. It was slightly racy, but viewers loved it. So did the company, which ended up advertising with us for several years.

One of the more challenging product placements was for an online sex-toy store, which was scheduled to run in one of the videos in the series where we built an off-grid Sprinter van. In the ad, I supposedly pulled a blurred-out dildo from the box it was shipped in—only it wasn't a dildo. Earlier that morning, I'd found a three-foot-long metal rod in the shop, and it stood in for the real thing.

I got some backlash about the ad, but surprisingly not from commenters. Instead, other YouTube car influencers complained, saying that they wouldn't accept the company as a sponsor in a million years. I don't know—maybe they were jealous that Adam & Eve didn't put some sex money in their pockets.

Then again, this wasn't my first rodeo selling sex online.

All the major car magazines and websites—*Car and Driver*, *Motor-Trend*, *Jalopnik*, and top-level columnists—have arrangements with car manufacturers to send them brand-new vehicles free of charge so they can drive the car around for a week and write a review. Makes sense. How can you write about a car if you haven't driven it?

In all my years of running the channel, I've never had a car manufacturer offer us a loaner to review. Of course, *Rich Rebuilds* is not your typical media outlet. Some manufacturers might be very hesitant to send us a car because of our reputation for off-color jokes, bleeped-out curse words, and doing multiple donuts in 7-Eleven parking lots. But we do have millions of loyal subscribers, and numerous videos have generated more than a million views.

I don't buy new cars, either for my own use or to feature on the channel, so admittedly I'm no help when it comes to promoting the latest models. But car companies still sell used cars in their showrooms, and that's one place where I could offer my opinion.

The whole time I produced videos on the BMW i8, I never once heard from the company, which I suppose is a good thing, considering I was never a target of theirs. In the last video of the i8 series, I was annoyed at how unhelpful customer service at BMW could be. Then again, when it comes to my editorial stance, I am an open book. After watching just one video, it's obvious that I'm not afraid to speak my mind, which is likely why the company never reached out.

Today, when someone gets bumped from a flight or their bag gets misplaced, they often go on Facebook, Twitter, or TikTok to complain, because it usually gets faster results than calling a toll-free number. Most people recognize the immense power of social media, especially when it shows a company in a negative light, so I thought my complaints would generate a response from BMW USA or at least an apology or acknowledgment on their own social media accounts.

Instead, crickets.

I'd never needed BMW's cooperation before, but now I needed them to make a new key for the car that I've been driving for years. But my complaints in the videos fell on deaf ears with BMW USA.

When I contacted BMW Germany, they responded immediately and shipped a new key directly to my door within a week. Sometimes it's your own people . . . funny how that works.

All this meant that if I wanted to test-drive a new car—and create some killer content in the meantime—I'd have to be proactive. My friend Josh started to reach out to companies on my behalf. One day he contacted Lucid and asked if they'd lend me a brand-new Air so I could make a video about it. At first they hesitated. Of course they didn't want us to bash the car or damage it in any way, but I laid down the law in the very beginning.

We told them, "Guys, you need to listen to me. You need to allow us to do the things that we do, and we need to be unfiltered because that's what viewers expect. We have to make fun of the car because *that's what we do.*"

They gritted their teeth, but they agreed.

We flew out to California to shoot the video "Elon Said It's a Dumpster Fire. We Will Find Out for You." We drove all around the area doing donuts, burnouts, and pushing the car to its breaking point.

Then the real fun started.

There's a section in the video where it looks like the Lucid staff members were having second thoughts about us putting the car through its paces and said we could continue as long as we had someone from the company chaperone us for the rest of the trip. So one of the employees climbed into the car and made faces as we drove.

In reality, Lucid actually had no problem with us pushing the car to its limits. We came up with the idea to add a chaperone while we were driving. It turns out that our video is one of the more popular review videos about the car to date. And Lucid loved it.

Viewers like to see when I succeed, but I think they want to see the times when I fail even more.

Oh sure, *Rich Rebuilds* shows people how to fix cars and learn about the inner workings of an automobile, but part of the appeal is both escapist and aspirational: *Hey, if that guy can drive a fancy Audi or Porsche, maybe I can too.*

Over the years, I've noticed that videos that have an extremely negative spin are the ones that pull in the most viewers. After all, many people love nothing more than to say, "Ha, I thought you wouldn't be able to pull that off, and you didn't!"

So when I made a video called "I Tried to Service My 700HP Audi RS7 Myself," I knew it would generate more views than usual. While they may not come right out and say it, some people will watch in order to make themselves feel better about owning a Ford Focus. To me, everything is content. I'm constantly viewing the world through the lens of an iPhone camera for future videos. Like I said, I can't turn off my brain.

Sometimes, I'll see something interesting and poignant, or funny and stupid, so I'll have no choice but to take out my iPhone to shoot a short clip because it might fit into a future video. In fact, what frequently happens is that a few months later, I'll be editing a video and suddenly remember that I have the perfect clip to tack on.

For instance, one day my son was getting out of the Porsche, and when he opened the door, it hit my Rivian pickup truck and left a scratch on the door.

I know, boo-hoo, first world problems.

I told him to be more careful next time and took a video of it and filed it away. A month later, I was making a video about the Rivian and thought, *This is perfect*, and slotted it right in.

Everything is content.

ONE HAND IN MY POCKET

I always have my wallet and my phone in my pocket. I don't have any keys. In fact, I haven't carried a key in probably a decade or more.

That's because I'm such a scatterbrain that I tend to lose everything. In fact, it's so bad that I keep a backup wallet at my house with twenty bucks, a spare credit card, and an ID in it. If I lose my wallet, I can just grab the replacement.

Instead of a key, my house has a fingerprint lock. I probably shouldn't say this, but when it comes to the cars, I usually leave the keys in them because *see above*. That's another reason I tend to wear black, gray, and dark blue clothes, because it's one less thing for me to think about.

———

UNCLE RICH'S RITALIN

I can't stop fixing things.

Fixing things grounds me, and it keeps me calm. Fixing things is my Ritalin. Whenever I look at something that's not working, I always think, *This isn't broken. The life for this is not over.* And I usually plunge right in to puzzle it out, because that's what keeps me calm and sane.

If I was a kid today, they'd definitely put me on some kind of drug. I'm convinced—as are many others—that I have ADHD. A friend once told me that he had ADHD too, and once he started taking Ritalin he was great, minus the migraines.

Minus the migraines? No thanks. I've thought about taking it, but I decided against it. I've made it this far in life without it, and I don't want it to change who I am. After all, if I did start focusing on things, would I be in the position that I am now? *A better, more productive version of myself,* you say? I don't know, and I don't really want to find out.

But I have to compensate for my scatterbrain somehow, so I wake up extremely early, around four, and do as many things as I can as inefficiently as possible, because that's how I roll. I give myself extra time to compensate for my scatteredness.

I am also a horrible vacationer. Not too long ago, I wanted to clear my head, so I hopped in my car and went to a beach and sat there and looked around at all the people lying in the sun. I'm thinking, *What the hell are you guys doing? There's a whole world out there!* I couldn't stand it and I couldn't sit still, so I found a discarded cup on the beach and started scooping sand so I could make a sandcastle. I can't just do nothing.

So yes, repairing stuff is great because it extends the life of something that would normally be thrown away, but I also need to do it for personal reasons. If I'm not fixing something, I can't function. Fixing things *is* my Ritalin.

CHAPTER SEVEN

FIGHTING THE TESLA MONSTER

When the Electrified Garage opened its doors in Seabrook, New Hampshire, in the spring of 2019, customers swarmed to the shop.

Business was brisk from day one, and there was some cross-pollination along the way as fans of the YouTube channel became fans of the garage and vice versa. We held a few open houses at the garage and appeared at community events and fairs, so more locals learned about the YouTube channel.

In the beginning, there were lots of people coming into the shop who were fans of the channel and specifically asked for me. Maybe they thought I filmed my videos there. Chad,

Chris, or one of the other employees would let them down easy by telling them that if I worked on their car, then I wouldn't have time to make videos.

I sometimes think that a lot of guys watch my videos in a voyeuristic way, because they don't understand why I never throw something across the room when I can't fix it in five minutes, which is what they would do.

Mechanics of all stripes—amateurs at home and professionals at the dealership—throw stuff in garages all the time. They get mad because they can't figure out why they can't fix something. I'll be the first to admit that working on cars can be frustrating. A car is expensive, so when it doesn't work and you're running out of money and time and you've got to get to your day job—well, sometimes it just feels good to throw a wrench against the wall.

I never get angry when I fix things. I think that's because I was raised by a house full of women who took a different approach to handling their problems. Whenever something broke, they didn't get mad. Instead, they viewed it as not a big deal and figured it would get resolved one way or another.

And they never took it personally.

So, most of the time, I don't throw something that could dent a wall or a car.

I said *most* of the time.

It all goes back to fixing that VCR. I just wanted to help my mom and aunts. Though, admittedly when I couldn't fix it, I stuffed it under the bed. Then again, I was very young. Even today, my curiosity drives me to keep going when I come up against a brick wall and really need to puzzle something out.

That's kind of how I felt with the Tesla stuff in the beginning. It was like a secret society because I couldn't find anyone who could help me. I felt if I just figured out the right password, I'd receive the keys to the Tesla kingdom.

While I am comfortable working on cars, I know that many people can't tell their oil fill from their windshield-wiper-fluid fill, nor do they want to. And that's okay. We decided to focus our business model for the Electrified Garage on helping people who felt confused or left out in the cold. Based on the response after we opened our doors, there were a lot of people out there who felt extremely helpless and misunderstood when it came to their Teslas, since the company wouldn't repair cars like Dolores, which had been written off due to insurance.

After the garage opened, I was only slightly surprised that we didn't hear from Tesla corporate directly. However, our local Tesla service center brought several of their employees to offer test-drives at our open house. While our local Tesla guys were great, it was obvious that corporate didn't exactly share their view. But, like most huge corporations, Tesla isn't a big fan of bad PR. If the Electrified Garage had been a tiny mom-and-pop shop that no one knew about, I'm pretty sure the company would have been more inclined to kick us around. After all, we did have two former Tesla employees on staff. But because we have a very big social media reach and millions of people know who we are, I think any pushback from Tesla would have created a media storm framed like David versus Goliath: the big bad company wants to shut down a tiny garage. This would get a lot of attention for them, and not the good kind.

Even though Tesla had been very good to me in terms of building my new life and career, and even though we were serving people who loved their Teslas, I was beginning to discover that there were many Tesla drivers out there who held very rigid views about the company.

To them, Elon Musk could do no wrong and the cars were without fault. Anyone who suggested otherwise deserved an outpouring of righteous indignation, because if you're attacking the car, you're attacking Elon. It's almost as if you're saying something against the Holy Father himself.

Since I was criticizing the company for its business practices, among other things, it didn't take long for these Tesla superfans to put me in their crosshairs. Case in point: I chronicled my experience buying a used Model X online and then driving it after it arrived. Over the course of four separate videos, I painstakingly detailed my experience, every misstep of the way, from describing how one rep told me they had no record of my purchase to receiving delayed and broken parts.

In 2019, when Elon Musk was well on his way to becoming the world's richest person, his mom tweeted a 1995 picture that showed her son crouching by his first car, a 1978 BMW. He was so broke that he had to fix it himself with parts from a junkyard. "And people said you knew nothing about cars," his mother tweeted.

Somewhere around fifty people messaged me about the tweet. I thought it was hilarious, because it was so ironic that once upon a time he actually thought it was a good idea for people to get parts for their cars from junkyards.

How times have changed.

As I am not an emotional guy by nature, I kept my voice neutral throughout the seven-video series I called "Model X Order Mess." I backed up everything on the video with receipts and photos of the damage to the car, as well as my correspondence with the company.

Many of the comments viewers left were along the lines of "I can't believe you went through that" and "My brand-new Model X has been in the shop six times in six months." But there was a small group of vocal commenters who complained about my complaints, telling me, "You should cut them some slack" and "Maybe you should have waited for the Model Y or just buy a new Tesla instead."

To me, these fanboys and -girls—or Musketeers, as I started to refer to them—were an interesting bunch, and I accepted them as part of the business of having some degree of online visibility. I admit that if Tesla had sold me parts from the very beginning, maybe my sentiment toward them would be better, but as the whole Model X debacle worsened, I began to voice my opinions about other things that I didn't like about the company.

Of course, that increased the ratio of negative to positive comments, with the underlying theme of "Why are you being so negative when Tesla has done so much for you?"

While I didn't defend myself—other viewers did that for me in the Comments section—I'll admit that I started spending way more time and energy addressing the conflict than I should have. After reading these comments day in and day out, I could literally feel the testosterone leaving my body. Then again, the ongoing skirmishes increased my viewership and subscriber numbers, because, after all, who doesn't like a good food fight, either online or IRL?

Part of me totally gets the Musketeers' concerns. After all, Elon's doing it all: he's building cool cars, digging tunnels, and going to space. Admittedly, many nerds have typically lacked significant role models in the past, and when one comes along who stays in the public eye for an extended period of time, it's tempting to latch on with the rest of the fist-pumping lemmings. However, when some rough-around-the-edges random guy starts talking slick about their commander in chief, well, they don't like it very much.

I was becoming somewhat of a villain in the Tesla community, and the Musketeers' number one complaint was that I was an anti-environmentalist and wanted the earth to go to hell. Why else would I say bad things about Musk and his company? After all, Tesla is perfect and so is Elon, since he's done so much for our environment. And he's sending us all to space, exploding rockets notwithstanding.

Their logic was that anyone who drives a gas-powered car is automatically a bad person who needs to be shamed and ostracized until they see the error of their ways. "Why are you buying anything that's powered by gas? You're hurting the environment. Don't you care about your children?" And since I was fixing Teslas instead of buying a new one, well, I'm the worst person in the world, because then I'm literally stealing money out of Elon's pocket. I was a gas-car-driving Tesla basher.

The irony is that I started to be known as the Tesla Guy in both news stories and in person. Whenever someone came up to me to say, "Hey, you're the Tesla Guy!" I always thanked them for watching the channel, but it was weird to be recognized. Some of them were clearly converts to the cause. They were so excited about Tesla that it felt like they had joined a cult.

In fact, I've seen this conversion firsthand, and it ain't pretty. I had one friend who really wanted a Model 3, but he couldn't afford it on his salary. So he stretched his finances to the point where he was able to buy one, but there was one small problem: he lived in a large apartment building and had no way of charging the vehicle. So every night before he went home, he had to sit at a charging station for up to an hour just to get enough charge so he could start the car the next day. I think he would've been a lot better off buying a Honda Civic or Accord, but he wanted to prove to total strangers that he had money, which was crazy because he really didn't.

Tesla has also done a great job of brainwashing people into thinking that by buying a Tesla they're automatically saving the planet from certain annihilation. What people don't understand—and I regularly blow people's minds when I tell them this, if they're willing to listen—is that if you

really want to be an environmentalist, then you are far better off keeping the things you already have and maintaining
them, taking public transportation or sharing a small, used,
fuel-efficient car or EV with a friend or neighbor, and living
within your means. After all, when you buy something new,
it requires additional resources in the form of mining raw
materials and metal, which sends more carbon and pollution
into the atmosphere.

In fact, it drives me crazy when people tell me that they're
saving the world just because they drive an electric car and
have solar panels on their house. That's great, but maybe
you wouldn't need so many solar panels if you didn't have a
ten-thousand-square-foot house and didn't have to charge your
three or four planet-saving Teslas all at the same time—not to
mention maintaining your generous acreage of nicely man-
icured lawn, ahem. I guess nobody told these people that
grass lawns and their upkeep come with massive carbon costs,
increase greenhouse gases, destroy ecosystems, waste water,
and are totally unsustainable. Keep in mind that your house
has to be heated and cooled, and in turn your five kids will
own more Teslas and buy large homes, only to further increase
their generation's carbon footprint. Technically, if you want
to really make the statement that you're saving the world,
you should downsize and just ride a bike, but nobody wants
to do that.

To the Musketeers, this was utter sacrilege. But it was com-
ical watching them go tit for tat on who's saving the environment harder. If they thought that your environment-saving

tactics weren't up to snuff, you were judged accordingly...I wish my stool was this soft.

In fact, the only place where the fanboys and -girls got it right was when they said I wasn't an environmentalist. Correct: I've never said that I was. I've always been very open about explaining that the reason I bought my first Tesla was not to save the planet but because it was cool and fast and provided me with a challenge because the technology was really new at the time.

Don't get me wrong. I am very conscious of the environmental impact that I have in the world. I try to do very basic things, like recycling and bringing reusable bags to the grocery store, and I always buy used cars and run them into the ground. It's when people say that they're helping the environment by buying a $100,000 car or designer biodegradable bags to hold their dog's shit that is just ludicrous. Have you tried downsizing? Does the AC have to be set at fifty in the summer for twenty-four hours a day?

And I'm the bad guy?

I just want to casually point out that Elon himself made over 120 trips in his private jet in 2022 alone, with some trips as short as six minutes. This is equal to the annual emissions of 375 cars, or heating and cooling 170 homes for a full year.

Obviously, the Musketeers didn't want to hear any of this, so instead they doubled down on trying to bury me with every new video I released. Whenever I said something the least bit critical of the company in a video, the number of negative comments skyrocketed and hundreds of people unsubscribed.

It's one thing to fight the manufacturer. Once I learned how Tesla operated, I started to view it as a challenge: *Okay, they won't sell me this part. How can I get it?* And I usually figured out a work-around.

But fighting the teeming hordes of extreme Tesla fans was something else entirely. I only wanted to educate people about the cars and what to expect from the company—that is, not much. Tesla liked to imply that their cars were so perfect that they never needed service, which of course was very far from the truth. So when I said in numerous videos that Tesla was wrong and their cars *do* need service—and good luck if you wanted an appointment sooner than three months in the future—the onslaught from the Musketeers felt like when the Ninja Turtle villain Krang sent out a giant hive mind of headless drones, all with the sole purpose of taking me down. They thought I relied on shame to keep my act together.

I knew something had to change.

I fought the Musketeers, for a while at least. I always try to fight a good fight, so I thought the best way to counter their arguments was to continue to painstakingly lay out detailed explanations in my videos, while adding a good dose of my snarky humor.

But then the company itself joined the pile on by pulling my access to their Supercharger network without warning. Instead of adding seventy-five miles of range in five minutes, I was demoted to standard charging, where a full charge could take hours. Next, the company zapped my referral credit—where I could earn thousands of dollars if a buyer ordered a Tesla and

My mother perched me on the hood of her 1982 Pontiac Firebird when I was about a year old.

According to my mother, when I was three years old my favorite things in the world were cars and trucks.

In the first video I ever posted to YouTube, I stole a plastic pink knife from my son's lunch box to scrape away the corrosion from Dolores's battery.

When I was thirteen years old, I was the epitome of cool... plus, I had hair.

I was the raisin in the oatmeal through all seven years at Saint Mary of the Hills (Catholic) School in Milton, Massachusetts.

In high school, I couldn't afford to buy designer clothes, so I scavenged discarded Nautica and Polo shirts, cut out the logos, and glued them to no-name shirts I bought at Building #19.

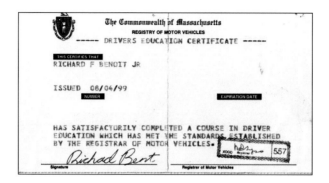

After I completed my Driver's Ed program, my life would never be the same.

Besides cars, my other favorite thing when I was a kid was my Texas Instruments TI-99 computer.

My mother holds me on the breakwater in Gloucester, Massachusetts, in 1985. Today, my shop is not far away in the same town.

Breanna, my first-born, provided me with lots of challenges when I became a teenaged father, but also lots of love.

Leenda Lucia provides a welcome boost to the channel. *Photo credit: Leenda Lucia*

My father and I
relaxing at home,
the nine-hundred-
square-foot ranch
where I grew up
in Mattapan,
Massachusetts.

Working in IT
wasn't only telling
employees how
to reboot their
computers; my
colleagues and I
also frequently
kicked back.

My dog Biscuit often uses my shoes
as a chew toy, and I'll wear them until
they're falling off my feet.

Apparently, I am the only Black owner of a Sherp in the entire United States who isn't a rapper or an entertainer in some way.

Building the world's first jet-powered hovercraft was one of my more unusual projects.

Working with Robert Downey Jr. on his HBO Max show *Downey's Dream Cars* was something I could have never imagined when I started my YouTube channel.

Sometimes you gotta make do with what's on hand to get the job done.

Sometimes a project needs prayer hands and vintage clothing to keep it all together.

entered my code—because they said my videos "acted in bad faith."

The irony is that hundreds of people were using my referral code to buy new Teslas, so wasn't the point of the code to help sell cars? If my videos were so bad for the company's image, then why were people still buying Teslas in droves?

My stress was off the charts, though I was always careful to keep it from seeping into my videos. There's a lot to be said for putting an old car up on jack stands and spending a few hours loosening bolts and nuts while rocks, dirt, and debris fall onto your face. Since I still had a few gas-powered cars in my garage, I could feel the tension drain out of my body as I wrenched away, and I was able to tune out the Tesla flame wars for at least a few hours.

To be perfectly honest, even if the Musketeers didn't exist, I was getting tired of working on Teslas. After all, I had been taking them apart and fixing them for several years now, and I knew how they ticked. At this point I had taken apart—and put back together—so many Teslas that I could do it in my sleep.

I felt like I'd said everything there was to say about electric vehicles in my videos, and I missed the challenge of working on a variety of cars. In my gut, I knew I couldn't make videos about Teslas anymore.

My love affair with Tesla was coming to an end.

I was at a crossroads. Up to that point, my whole universe was Tesla stuff. It's why over half a million people had subscribed to my channel by the end of 2019. I wanted to start making videos about gas-powered cars. I thought I could succeed since even today the number of gas vehicles on the road vastly over-shadows EVs.

I also wanted to continue to grow my YouTube audience. I'd already seen numerous YouTubers crash and burn from going on automatic pilot from the endless cycle of cranking out new videos each week, with viewership tanking as a result. I knew I couldn't fake it. If I did, I'd face the same fate.

I was terrified. But in my gut, I knew I couldn't do Tesla stuff anymore.

I decided to test the waters with another car, a hybrid.

Baby steps.

SAY UNCLE

Uncle Rich came about because someone called me that one day as a joke and it just kind of stuck.

After all, Uncle Rich has a certain ring to it. I also like how it sounds and the meaning it conveys: I'm your uncle, not an annoy-ing family member who lives in your house and who you have to deal with every day. Instead, I'm that guy you see every week or so in a video. You probably don't see your uncles very often, but you know they're there. And when you see them, they're friendly and probably pretty funny.

I started referring to myself as Uncle Rich partly as a joke but also to put people at ease. When I was a kid, my father had nick-names like Defribbits and Fringo, which I thought were funny. But what's hilarious is that he gave me a variation of his nicknames as my actual middle name.

So I wanted a nickname too. I've always liked the idea of being the cool uncle, so when I started having nieces and nephews of my own, my relatives would tell them, "Go say hi to Uncle Rich," and it kind of grew from there. I don't normally call myself Uncle Rich, but sometimes I'll say something in a video like "Hey, Uncle Rich is here for you" as a kind of gag.

HEY, YOU'RE THE TESLA GUY!

Everyone thinks if you have success, fame, and money that you're going to have women chasing you down the street, but that couldn't be further from the truth. I don't have a single female groupie. It's all guys. I'm not complaining about my audience, just setting expectations here.

Sometimes guys will see me and totally freak out and scream, "Oh my God, it's you!" which is really embarrassing. I tell them that I'm just a regular, down-to-earth guy and that I have my assistant put on my pants like everyone else, but that usually doesn't stop them from gushing, "I can't believe it's you! I can't believe you're talking to me!"

I can't figure it out: Why *wouldn't* I talk to you? My kids think it's hilarious that I get stopped all the time, while my wife just rolls her eyes.

One day I was picking up dinner at a Five Guys and a fan caused a scene like I was the pope. To be fair, I don't think the pope drives a Tesla.

I said, "Buddy, take it down a notch. I'm just a regular guy."

He insisted on paying for my meal, which I said was a very respectful gesture, but I wanted to buy my own meal. But he kept pushing it, so finally I said if he wanted to support me, keep watching the videos, and he said, "No problem."

For a while, whenever someone recognized me and said, "Hey, you're the Tesla Guy!" I wanted to ask, "When's the last time you watched one of my videos? What year do you think we're in?" After all, I did my last Tesla build in 2020, when I gave all my Tesla stuff away. And to me, the V8 Tesla doesn't count.

Part of me is flattered because I got my footing there, and I will never dismiss the fact that Tesla is what gave me my claim to fame. But it's a tough thing to shake, and I don't think I'll ever be able to, so instead of getting annoyed, I've started to embrace it. After all, that's how people know me. So today, whenever someone calls me the Tesla Guy, I shake their hand, pose for a photo, and say, "Thank you very much." I always take the time to talk to a fan for a few minutes, sometimes upward of an hour.

Probably the strangest place I've been recognized was when my buddy Sean and I went to a rodeo in Texas, and a guy slowed down and asked, "Are you from YouTube?" This was one of the first times I was recognized, and I only had about forty thousand subscribers at the time, but that made me feel good. Uncle Rich has made it, baby. There are even people in Texas looking for me.

Yeehaw.

CHAPTER EIGHT

THE BACKLASH

Despite the behavior of the Musketeers, I never held anything against Elon himself, at least not in the beginning. After all, in some ways, we are very much alike, and in some ways we are better or equal to each other.

For example, he's always been an entrepreneur who's willing to take huge risks. Indeed, Tesla was a huge risk that paid off in the end. I bought my multifamily properties fully knowing they were a big risk, and they've proved to be a good investment. Tesla is much more lucrative, so one point for Elon.

I like to think I'm a reasonably smart individual, but there are lots of people far smarter than I am. Elon is also a highly intelligent man, but sometimes he speaks above people's heads since he has a much more technical mindset. I can talk the tech talk to the nerds, of course—after all, I am one—but my videos are aimed at the everyman. One point for Rich.

I think I'm a better communicator than he is. When I went on the *Joe Rogan* show, Joe explained how difficult it was to interview Elon back in 2018. Later, I watched the interview and saw that he did have a hard time formulating his thoughts. Maybe it was due to nerves, or maybe he's always the one in charge so he was thrown when the tables were turned. I don't know. But based on the poster hanging on the wall of my garage, it was clear that he smoked marijuana on the show to calm his nerves. That, combined with the fact that we both have multiple children, at least one ex-wife, and two hands and feet, we are basically the same person. Tied.

For years, he was the underdog, a brilliant Silicon Valley kid. He was young, goofy-looking, and a nerd. People could relate. Plus, back then he had no hair, but then suddenly he had hair again. Maybe it grew back out of respect? Mine never grew back, so one point for Elon.

After the hair came back, he started making some crazy moves. Today, I think he believes that he's untouchable, and perhaps he is, but at times the little Silicon Valley kid seems to have gone off the deep end. One point for Rich.

I suppose that one or two hundred billion will do that to you... funny how that works.

That's where we differ. I always bend over backward to respect everyone, from colleagues, friends, and family to total strangers. If anything, I usually go overboard, which is a leftover from childhood, when I had to prove to my white class-mates that not every Black guy is like the ones they watched on TV.

I don't think he gets enough credit for this, but Elon is a great visionary and a genius engineer. At the very least, he knows to hire the good ones. He's also a great front man for the marketing machine.

Elon likes to push the envelope to see what he can get away with, just like I do. But at this point, I think that a lot of his drama is driven by his ego. After all, when you're the richest man in the world several times over, what do you do next?

Apparently, you start saying crazy stuff.

Another way we're different.

Mostly.

My next envelope-pushing move would prove to be a delicate bal-ancing act. Even though there was no love lost between the Musketeers and me, I didn't want them to unleash their venom.

For my first non-Tesla project, I chose a BMW i8, a hybrid sports car that can operate on either gas or electricity. It's a plug-in hybrid, so you get the best of both worlds, which would project to the Musketeers that it's totally fine, no need to worry, nothing to see here.

After all, I wasn't doing anything crazy, like working on a 100 percent gas-powered car.

Unlike with Tesla, I could buy any BMW part that I needed, but they didn't come cheap. After all, BMW is not known for their low prices for cars, parts, or service. Most of the parts I needed ran about $1,000 each, and it hurt—a lot—every time I had to shell out the money. In fact, working on the i8 was the most expensive build I had done up to that point, and I couldn't purchase another parts car because there were already so few of them on the road.

In fact, I was lucky to find a salvaged i8 for about $25,000. A brand-new one ran about $150,000 at the time. But for me, an inveterate cheapskate, these were crazy prices. I didn't like spending that kind of money, because after you buy a certain number of parts, you could've just bought another car, though not an i8 of course. But it didn't much matter since the i8 was quickly turning into one of my favorite builds.

First, everyone loves this car. The i8 looks a lot more expensive than it really is. Plus, it is ridiculously easy to work on because all the body panels are made of plastic, so it is like working on Legos or an Erector Set. Swapping out parts was a dream because everything made sense and snapped right into place.

When I first got Dolores, I was in totally foreign territory and everything was new to me. Even though the i8 was a hybrid with an electric motor, I was back on familiar ground. Besides, if I could work on a Tesla, I could work on anything. The prospect for danger was also greatly reduced since the i8's battery is a lot smaller and harder to access. I hired someone to weld some tabs back onto the suspension, but other than that, I did all the work on the car myself in the same exact place in my garage where I had worked on Dolores.

For years, whenever I had to deal with Tesla, I felt like I was living in the movie *Scott Pilgrim vs. the World*, where I had to prove my worth by working my way up the ladder before they'd sell me a part. First, I had to fistfight three men, then wrestle an alligator, and finally deal with a mind-control device before they'd deem me worthy enough to take my money, and sometimes not even then.

As a result, I was so accustomed to having to lie, cheat, and steal to get parts for my Teslas that I kept a few gas-powered cars on the side just to avoid the abuse. For those cars, if I couldn't find a part at my usual sources, I called the dealership and gave them the VIN and my credit card information. Sometimes I'd hesitate and think of asking, "Aren't you going to punch me in the face?"

Pause. "Why would we do that?"

"Because you're going to tell me that my car is salvage and I'm not smart enough to work on the car myself and it poses a risk to others that are on the road."

Longer pause. Then, "Do you want the parts or not?"

I moaned like a gazelle in the southern Himalayas. I was finally back in the world of the living.

A few years ago, I shot some video that showed at least twenty wrecked Teslas sitting in someone's yard. It killed me to see the end product of tens of thousands of hours of engineering and all those lithium-ion batteries leaching into the earth. If the company would just give people—and other mechanics—the tools, information, and parts to fix their own cars, then we could avoid a yard full of environmentally hazardous cars that are just rotting away.

I once watched a documentary about Cuba that showed how the citizens have kept their cars on the road for decades, since importing new cars became essentially illegal in 1960 unless the government gave you permission. As a result, drivers learned how to keep their cars running as long as possible, usually with duct tape and chicken-wire fixes. While I don't agree with the overall principles of Communism, I want to point out that *this* is what being environmentally conscious looks like: reusing what you have and deciding to not buy a new car every two years because you're bored with your current model. And it most certainly doesn't mean buying a six-figure electric car.

In other words, don't be that guy who buys an electric car that sits in the driveway while he works from home.

Tesla likes to brag that they're an earth-friendly company, but by not selling parts to owners, they refuse to acknowledge the huge environmental benefit of decentralized repair by owners and local businesses. If Tesla believes that only they are capable of fixing their own cars, how is that sustainable?

When I tried—and failed—to fix my mom's VCR, even the smallest town had a shop that fixed most household appliances, everything from TVs to refrigerators and washing machines.

Today those shops are long gone, owing to so-called advances in mass production and marketing that make almost everything disposable. In most cases it's cheaper to buy a new stove or TV than to buy the parts to fix it yourself, even if you have the skills. We live in a society where the information that people need to fix their own things simply doesn't exist, or if it exists, the availability of a replacement is ubiquitous. Just try to find a parts catalog or repair manual these days. Most manufacturers don't even issue them anymore, and if they do, they're buried online or behind a paywall. A booming business nowadays is pirating these catalogs and manuals and selling them to the masses at a discounted rate.

Reminds me of a past life... 😊

I've always believed consumers should have the opportunity to fix their own things. Appliance and car manufacturers don't want you to fix your own stuff; they want you to buy something new because that means more money in their pockets. Most don't care about the environmental impact, because they don't have a program to recycle your old crap.

As a lifelong rebuilder, this just galls me.

For this reason, I've publicly protested about the way Tesla conducts its business when it refuses to sell parts to individuals. After all, most states have Right to Repair laws, which require auto manufacturers with dealerships in a state to sell parts to consumers. Tesla got around this by claiming these Right to Repair laws didn't apply to them, since they didn't have physical dealerships. After all, the only way you can buy one of their cars is online.

I had to get involved, for myself and for others. I was very happy when some Electrified Garage customers told me they wanted to learn how to work on their own cars, so I lobbied people in the Massachusetts state government for a ballot initiative to broaden—and strengthen—the Right to Repair law in the state. Of course, the automotive industry spent tens of millions of dollars on ads to convince residents to vote against it, but in 2020 75 percent of residents voted for the revamped Right to Repair law. Tesla is now required to provide individual owners and independent garages with the information and tools to fix the cars themselves. Massachusetts drivers are no longer shackled to Tesla service centers.

I feel proud that I was able to help start what I hope can be a revolution in our consumer culture. But it's far from over.

I launched a series of videos on the i8, which were pretty well received. The Musketeers voiced their disapproval, but this time it was muted.

I noticed an interesting side effect. Now that I wasn't thinking about and working on Teslas 24-7, I started to relax, on camera and off. Of course, I usually winged it when it came to shooting the videos, but with the i8 something clearly shifted.

It may surprise some of you, but I'd rather be anywhere than in front of a camera. I hate looking at myself on video. I absolutely hate it. I don't like looking at my face; I don't like seeing any of my weird mannerisms. All I can focus on are all the mistakes I'm making, from the excessive eye blinks to the endless parade of ohs, ums, and whatevers. So after I edit a video and watch it when it goes live, I never look at it again.

I think it goes back to childhood. I always strove to become what others wanted me to be or thought I was. Somewhere along the line, I realized that I really didn't know who I was and what I wanted. I've never wanted to disappoint anybody, so I've always molded myself to make other people comfortable—if I'm around white people I act white, and if I'm around Black people I act Black—so I've never really asked myself, *Who am I? Who am I, really?*

I realize this all sounds strange coming from someone who has millions of subscribers on YouTube, but one day someone posted a comment that stopped me in my tracks.

"I think Rich's so confusing that he's lost himself. He's not even sure anymore who he really is."

When I read that, I thought, *Holy shit, he's right. How did he know?* Was this my unconscious writing in the Comments section again?

I'd been hiding behind Rich the character because it felt more comfortable than showing the real Rich. I'd gotten so caught up in the excitement of quitting my job, building a business, and experiencing newfound fame that I was starting to feel a bit dislocated. Had I gotten so lost in my character that I didn't know who I was anymore? Had I actually *become* that character?

I've long tried to balance a fine line and edit in my head while we're shooting. I think of something funny to say, but then I don't because I don't want to offend anyone.

But then I think, *Oh wait, I'm shooting a video. People are watching me.* So then I give them the me that I think they want, which isn't always me, because I think if they got the real me, then they wouldn't like him, because he's not very social, he's too sarcastic, and he loves dark humor. After all, it's like food: not everybody has the same taste. If you look at my very early videos, you'll see more of the constipated me, constantly nervous to really let that character come out.

So receiving that comment was a very humbling moment. Am I that person, or am I just pretending that I'm that person so I could *be* that person? In a way, I'm doing the same thing I did when I was a kid and took apart everything in my house so I could figure things out. It calms me down, of course, and helps me focus, but I don't really find the answer.

I've discovered that as I've gotten into the rhythm of having to produce a new video every week, I've gotten very good at playing these roles. And there's a certain point where I don't think that I'm playing a role anymore. I think that's just who I am. I think my true, real self is starting to come out in the videos.

So I've started to let my hair down a little bit more, so to speak. In one video I shot in early 2023, I basically said that if you're under fifty and have a gold watch, that's dumb. I also said that I think chiropractors are fake. I just said out loud how I felt instead of pushing it down. I normally wouldn't do that, because then I imagine a national chiropractic association coming down on me, or that some random forty-year-old guy with a gold watch his grandfather gave him is going to come crying in the Comments. Or better yet, I said to the people who invite me to their birthday parties, *I don't want to go to your birthday party.* Birthday parties are like penises: I like my own, and that's it.

But no one said anything. In fact, some people told me that they felt the same way, so it was a huge validation for me. Before, I would always use sarcasm or an alternate persona to express those beliefs.

The next video I'd release would really stir the pot, changing not only the course of the channel but my entire career.

MY BINKY

I love my cars, and I love my binky.

Believe it or not, I have a blanket that I bring almost everywhere with me. It brings me comfort. When I was a kid, I had an old blanket that was brown and had a giant horse on it. It had pilled and gotten pretty threadbare over the years, but it didn't matter because I loved that blanket. I ended up losing it somewhere along the way, and even though it was a mess, I was inconsolable.

A few years ago, someone made a blanket for one of the kids that had ducks printed all over it. My kids didn't seem to be that interested in it, so I stole it. It had that same kind of pilled texture as my childhood blanket, and as I used it more and more, it started to remind me of that lost blanket.

I'll bring it with me when I'm traveling, since hotel blankets aren't that great, or at least that's what I tell myself. In a way, it's like having a favorite pillow. I also like to have it next to me when I'm talking on the phone or editing videos. I never wash it, and I'm sure it smells like hot-dog water, but it's not that big of a deal.

I'm okay not having it. I mean, I could go weeks without it and be fine. In late 2022, I was on the road for three weeks and didn't bring it with me, but when I came back home, I thought, *Ah, there you are.* There were flies buzzing around it when I returned.

I'm over forty years old, so maybe I should be embarrassed, but this blanket brings me a lot of comfort and helps keep the mean people in the Comments section away.

Plus, it keeps my bald head very warm in winter.

———

AMERICA'S FINEST

We filmed one episode of *Downey's Dream Cars* at a military base in California to test if the electric pickup truck that we built for Robert Downey Jr. could pull a tank, a trailer, and a semi, which in total was about a hundred tons. The truck was designed to pull three tons, and we succeeded, so we more than pulled it off.

During the taping, I said my lines and explained the work that I had done on the truck, but I couldn't keep my eyes off the soldiers, because to me they all looked like children.

My brother was a Marine for many years. He went to war and lost friends in combat. How do you ever recover from that? You don't. When he was overseas, one of the safest places was in a bunker. It was the only place where he felt safe.

Today he's retired from the military, but the war never really left him. He works as a semitruck driver and drives all across the United States. He spends hours each day in a really small, confined space, but it's where he feels most comfortable. He also has a very small room in his house where he spends a lot of time, playing video games and relaxing.

When we were done filming, I shook hands with these kids. Yes, *kids*. They didn't even have facial hair. "Hey, man, love the channel," they told me. "I can't believe you're here."

It felt really surreal that they looked up to me. "Hey, guys," I replied. "Thanks for saving my ass, because I couldn't do what you guys do."

CHAPTER NINE

JUMPING SHIP

A lot of people want to see me fail.

Some people are just bored and they don't like the fact that I'm doing something cool. Or else they say I didn't go to school to build weird cars, that I'm not certified. Sometimes, it's sheer jealousy.

Of course, some of it is because some people think that Black people aren't supposed to work on cars, particularly on high-end luxury cars.

So I knew I was taking a huge risk when I posted the video "Why I'm Selling My Tesla and Going Back to Gas" on July 1, 2020—and sure enough, within hours, all hell broke loose.

Apparently, a large group of viewers complained to You-Tube in droves, claiming that the video "violated community standards," so YouTube took the video down. It was quickly reposted after they realized I hadn't done anything wrong, but a few hours later it got pulled a second time.

To this day, I still don't know who complained, and YouTube never told me, but I believe that a group of Tesla superfans had had enough of my antics and decided they wanted to punish me.

In the week that followed, die-hard Tesla and EV fans unsubscribed by the thousands and posted countless denunciations in the Comments section of my other videos. But they were just as quickly replaced by new viewers who welcomed the information I delivered along with my snark and humor. After all, while the content might have changed, *I* didn't change. My viewership and subscriber numbers actually went up.

Almost immediately, the difference was palpable, especially in the Comments section, which morphed from "You suck because you're killing the planet!" to "Well, you did it *this* way, but I would have done it *that* way."

Which was a clear improvement in my book.

From the first days of *Rich Rebuilds*, I realized that part of the deal is that I gain and lose subscribers all the time. It's an ebb and flow, where new people discover the channel for the first time while others lose interest and unsubscribe. No matter what I post, I typically lose a couple hundred subscribers per video.

While I was initially bummed at those figures, after online news outlets like *Vice* and the *Drive* covered the conflict, a lot of gas-powered aficionados tuned in to see what all the fuss was about and ended up subscribing to the channel. I gained well north of a hundred thousand new subscribers in just two months, which was significantly higher than before. In fact, the year after I stopped making videos about Tesla, the channel averaged about one thousand new subscribers a day.

All of this makes total sense, since the audience of Tesla and EV drivers was and still is very small compared to the number of people who drive gas-powered cars. For instance, there are maybe a million Teslas on the road today, while Toyota produces about a million Camrys in just a couple of years, so casting a wider net was definitely the way for me to go.

Not only did the channel grow, but so did I. I felt vindicated because I no longer had to force myself to do what others expected of me. I also felt freer to pursue the projects I was interested in, and that freedom resulted in me feeling more relaxed on camera, which then attracted even more viewers.

It was a huge lesson: I could do what I wanted and not destroy what I'd already built.

A few weeks later, I released a video called "I'm Giving All My Tesla Stuff Away," which didn't get flagged or pulled, probably because by then the Musketeers had totally given up on me.

In the video, I talked about how I was done with Tesla but that I wanted to give something back to the community for supporting me and helping me build my channel. So I told my loyal followers who had stuck by me to come get what was essentially tens of thousands of dollars' worth of parts and equipment for free.

They came, they got it, and two weeks later they were selling it on eBay.

I have to admit it was a huge blow. This is how you treat the person who gives you free entertainment and now free parts? You just turn around and sell it? I may be naive, but I've always been an optimist who chooses to see the best in people. With that one move, I suddenly saw how the world really works, and it wasn't as nice of a place as I had thought.

But I chalked it up to experience and turned to my next video, which had the potential to absolutely make or break me.

"**Why I Ditched My Tesla** for a Neglected Audi RS7" went live on August 2, 2020. It was my first fully gas-powered, post-Tesla video, so I braced for impact.

I've always wanted an RS7 because it's extremely loud and extremely fast, two of my favorite things. It was a gas-powered vehicle—maybe nine miles a gallon tops—so the Musketeers definitely would have viewed it as one giant middle finger to the environment, but since they had already unsubscribed in droves, I didn't have to worry.

I wasn't happy about the fact that the cars I was featuring on the channel were getting more expensive. The RS7 cost about $15,000 more than the i8. I had purchased the car from my friend Sam, who runs a YouTube channel called *Samcrac*. Like me, he buys cars and fixes them up to make video content. He made a few videos about the RS7 before deciding that he was done with it.

When I first looked at it, the car had been stored outside and was covered with dried grass and dust. There was a snake in the car and a couple of tree frogs in the trunk. It was right out of a horror movie, which created a pretty intense flashback to the smell of rotting fish when Dolores first showed up in my driveway.

The Audi hadn't been driven in six months since Sam had finished making a few videos on the car, so when I started it up, the engine wouldn't stop misfiring and was throwing codes for everything. But I didn't care. It was a beautiful vehicle and I knew I had to have it. In a way, I viewed it like a dog that had been neglected and needed a good home: I'll take a lot better care of it than Sam ever did. He had far too many cars to care about this one. Plus, it would make for great content. So we worked out a deal and I shipped the car back home.

I started working on the RS7 almost immediately, but I'd learned from the Smart car and didn't say anything about it to my followers until I was a couple of months into the project, especially since the Audi would be the first fully gas-powered car I'd feature on the channel.

I quickly realized that the RS7 was a good project for me personally because it taught me how to do more complex repairs, like bodywork, which I'd never done before. Though the car had a smashed-in floorpan, some people wouldn't have bothered fixing it, because once you put the matting for the rear trunk over the pan, you can't see it. But personally I couldn't drive that car knowing it was in that condition, let alone sell it to someone else in the future.

Besides, I like to do things that most people wouldn't attempt, on YouTube or not. So after I did some research, I thought, *I've certainly tackled more difficult projects. Why can't I do this?*

I bought all the parts and specialty tools I needed, along with a manual, and cut out the entire floorpan. Then I replaced the pan, sealed it, and painted it. I think I actually did a better job than the body shop that had worked on it before.

Plus, of course, my favorite thing: I had learned something new.

The next job was far more discouraging.

The RS7 has turbo oil screens that filter and strain oil. If you have an RS7 and need one replaced, brace yourself for the bill: Since Audis have massive engines and two large turbochargers, the manufacturer has to squish everything into a very small space. So it's impossible to get to the oil screen without having to first remove several components. It's easily a ten-hour job at the dealership, and you'd be lucky to get away with paying $1,800 for labor alone.

Have I mentioned how cheap I am? It was a very daunting task, but I decided to replace the screens myself, and once I started, I had to finish because that Audi was essentially dead in my garage until I completed the work.

I cursed, scraped my knuckles, and dropped parts on my feet, but the RS7 made me realize that I was far more capable than I had thought. I could do bodywork and perform a complex, daylong job that trained technicians are far better suited to handle.

And I did it all by myself.

One of the frustrations I always had with my Teslas was that I couldn't upgrade them. After all, I'm old-school: as soon as I get a car with some power, I want to modify it, add more power, and make it my own. The whole time I worked on Teslas, I felt like I had bought a house and couldn't paint the walls or change the decor.

Once I'd finished the repairs on the RS7, I started the modifications. I installed a tuner on it to make it faster and added a performance exhaust. I put bigger wheels on it. Then I launched that first video, "Why I Ditched My Tesla for a Neglected Audi RS7," and braced for impact.

I considered that first RS7 video as a kind of litmus test for the future. Could I finally break away from Tesla and do something different?

In the first few days, the video racked up double the number of views of my last noncontroversial Tesla video, and though a few trolls popped up here and there, viewers raved about the car, the channel, and my sense of humor, which was a total game changer.

Maybe this isn't about Tesla stuff after all. Maybe people are watching because of *me*.

Based on that one video, the answer was definitely yes. I made seven videos about the RS7 in all, and that series was one of my most successful to date.

Almost immediately, I felt the difference.

Instead of getting raked over the coals by the Musketeers, the worst comments I got were along the lines of: "You did this wrong, and I would have done it this way, but it worked so it doesn't matter." That's it. And I didn't have to fight anyone in the Comments section. As a result, my energy was different and I loosened up on camera.

I could do this forever.

I took a huge risk when I said that I don't have to be bound to Tesla, that I'm going to make the content that *I* want to make and take my chances.

I was finally rebuilding *me*.

Once the channel started to become successful, a lot of personal issues I had pushed down for years began to surface. I felt as if I didn't deserve much of the success I was achieving. And it started to spill over into my family life, so I decided to see a therapist.

The great thing about fixing stuff is you get instant feedback as to whether it's working or not. Well, this doesn't work, so let's try something else. The fact that I can have a result within a specific time frame that I've set myself has always amazed me, so I tend to view most things in life through a prism of measurable outcomes. I figured therapy would be the same way.

On the other hand, given my lifelong distrust of authority figures and teachers, I fully expected therapy to be a disaster. As it turned out, it was a bit of a mix.

First, of course, came the power struggle: Why should I listen to you? And what makes you qualified to listen to me? What are your credentials? Are you African American? Married? Do you have kids?

I was dismayed to find out that, unlike making videos and bringing cars back from the dead, when it came to therapy, measurable results were nowhere in sight. All I wanted to know is *When do I get fixed?* I was a classic "resistant" therapy client.

Eventually, I calmed down a little as the therapist said some insightful things that helped give me perspective and advice. I learned to resolve some of my issues on my own, but I recognize that having others tell me what to do will probably be a lifelong struggle for me. Now, when I encounter it, I've developed some coping mechanisms to make it less of an issue for me.

TALKING TO MYSELF

I really like to write, and over the last couple of years I've started to do more of it. But instead of actually writing things down, I talk to myself and create voice messages. I started doing it because I do a lot of voice-over work for my videos. I'll talk for five or ten minutes in the intro, and it's like thinking out loud.

A few times a week, I'll talk for fifteen minutes or so just to hear my own thoughts. It's not for a video but mostly so I can see the current state of my mind. It's like my diary.

When I get sad, I'll ask, *Why am I sad right now?* and then I'll just go off on a tangent. I also create these messages before I make a major decision. I'll talk about everything that's going on in my head and then play it back so I can hear how I sound to make sure my message is clear. Do I sound crazy? How am I coming across, and what's my tone? It also helps to hear from the listener's perspective.

———

BABY, YOU CAN DRIVE MY CAR

I love to share my cars with others so they can feel what I feel when driving them. If someone wants to go for a ride in the Sherp, I'll take them for a ride. If someone wants to see what it's like to drive the Hellcat or even the Rivian, I'll give them the keys and tell them to go enjoy themselves for a couple of weeks. I enjoy sharing things with people because when I was a kid—and even when I was in my twenties—I would have loved to have someone share their car with me. So I want to pay it forward.

After I finished rebuilding a Dodge Hellcat in 2023, I put maybe two miles on it. It's fun to drive, but honestly the car is kind of ridiculous. It has a ton of power, makes a ton of noise, and isn't fuel efficient. But I love seeing other people enjoy it and feel like it's a way to reward my colleagues for their hard work. Everyone on staff has been driving the car and beating the absolute crap out of it, going sideways and doing burnouts. They always come back grinning and say, "That was awesome."

That's what makes me happy.

CHAPTER TEN

DWB*

Now, I don't normally like to bring these topics up, but as a successful African American man living in the Northeast, the reaction I get from people tends to vary, and in this chapter I'll describe just a few examples of what I experience on a regular basis: Raking the yard. Doing my taxes. Eating ice cream.

All. While. Black.

Eighty percent of the time, I walk around looking like I'm homeless.

I usually wear shorts or dirty jeans because that's what's lying around. At any given point in time, there's a good chance that I've just worked on a car in the last hour or two, so I'm

---

* Dictionary.com defines DWB—aka Driving While Black—in this way: "Used ironically to refer to the stopping of a Black motorist by police because of the motorist's skin color rather than for any real offense."

probably at least a little dirty. One day, I wore my kid's shirt because all of mine were too gross.

My dog Biscuit likes to use my sneakers as a chew toy, but I wear them because, after all, they still serve their purpose. I have a closet full of never-worn, twenty-year-old fashion sneakers like Nike and Adidas that serves as a shrine to my lost childhood. Fans have sent me brand-new sneakers, and once I got a pair of Crocs in the mail with a note that said, "You don't have to live like this." I wore them a couple of times, even when I found out they're actually knockoffs. Truthfully, I still break them out every once in a while.

In public, the real disconnect comes when people see me getting into or out of a car that a rich white doctor would drive. My friends always made fun of me for this. They said that when I got the Hellcat, it was much more fitting, since the stereotype is that only Black people from Atlanta drive Hellcats. Fun fact: I purchased my Hellcat from Atlanta. But I don't know a single Black person who has a Porsche 911 or a Corvette Z06. That's one of the interesting things about living in the Northeast: if you want to meet fellow successful Black people, you have to drive about nine hours south.

When I was young, someone told me if I tinted my car windows, it would make the car feel like less of a fishbowl. I liked that idea when I first started to drive, because it meant if I happened to cut someone off by accident—or on purpose—when they pulled up next to me to stare me down, they couldn't see who was driving. But I also think that tinted windows make any car look better.

Today all my cars have tinted windows. I like to joke that, this way, whenever I'm pulled over, I'll know that it's because I screwed up and not because of my skin color.

On the other hand, I like to show people that it's perfectly normal for a guy like me to drive a car that's usually driven by guys that don't look like me... if you know what I mean. I also want to show kids that if they dream of driving an expensive car in the future, they can make it happen. So whenever I go somewhere like Home Depot, I always park my car in the far reaches of the parking lot. Partly because I don't want it to get dinged but also because I want people to know that, hey, we can have nice things too.

I've always had a high degree of self-awareness. I can always tell when I'm being followed, which has been the case my entire life. Someone will see me walk out of Home Depot and head toward a very expensive car with no other cars around it. Do they think I'm going to break into it? I don't go there, but whoever's following me will slow down and watch me approach the car.

When I unlock the car and get in, I smile and wave at the guy. He always looks away before driving off in the opposite direction, pretending that he got lost or made a wrong turn. You know, maybe I *should* start dressing better.

Welcome to my world.

Of course, people's initial perceptions of me are not limited to the Home Depot parking lot. I wish they were. I once was inside the store to buy a fridge for one of my rental units. It cost a couple thousand bucks, and the sales guy asked if I wanted to do a payment plan. I said no and handed him my credit card.

He looked at me and said, "That's a lot of money on a credit card. Most people usually put it on a payment plan."

I told him I'd put it on the credit card and pay it off at the end of the month. Then he asked what kind of house it was going to, and I said a rental property.

I saw the gears turning in his head: this (Black) person is buying an expensive fridge for a property he doesn't even live in.

Then the questions started.

They always start.

How long have you owned the property?

When did you get it?

How were you able to get it?

What do you do for work?

Would he ask a white person these questions? Maybe if they were twelve... But if he was honest, he should have just asked me this instead: *Why do you get to have this and I don't?*

Whenever I go out into the world and interact with strangers, I hear some form of this pretty regularly. When I bought my Sherp, it got even worse.

A Sherp is an off-road tank used in extreme conditions to rescue people and shuttle equipment. It's made in Ukraine and named after the Sherpas who transport equipment up and down Mount Everest; they can go everywhere and so can the Sherp. The tires inflate and deflate by pushing a button inside the cab.

It can also float in water.

I'd wanted one for a very long time, and it wasn't until I bought my own that I found out that apparently every African American who owns a Sherp is either a rapper or entertainer. Chris Brown has one. So do Joyner Lucas and 2 Chainz. Kanye West owned seven of them, but I don't know if Kim got any in the divorce.

Whenever I drove it, everyone automatically assumed I was famous, which was bittersweet. On the one hand, I was flattered that they would think that someone like me—skinny and under six foot one—could be an athlete or an entertainer. Then again, on that last point, I suppose I am.

But why did they think that I couldn't be an engineer? Why can't a guy like me who looks like he makes a good living be something other than a rapper? Once, someone actually asked me my name and what my SoundCloud was.

Even the company that sold me the Sherp assumed I was in the business. When I had a question about a minor repair, I called the company and spoke with a rep who answered it. When we were finished, he proceeded to ask me about my career in rap and said that I sounded familiar, which was odd since all my friends describe my voice as whiter than a bag of marshmallows.

Apparently, I am the only African American in the entire country with a Sherp who isn't a rapper or in the entertainment business in some way. Perhaps this is my own fault. Fun fact: I purchased the same Sherp that I saw 2 Chainz driving in a demo video.

Fun fact number two: 2 Chainz, Kevin Hart, and Jay Leno have all signed the kick panel of my Sherp.

Admittedly, the Sherp attracts a lot of attention, and I usually get pulled over when I'm driving it. While it doesn't have tinted windows, it *is* a tank, so people outside can't see who's inside. One day I took my kids out in the Sherp and we headed for the ocean. We went into the water and were floating near these super-expensive oceanfront houses when a family who lived in one of them waved us over. I pulled up on their private beach, and when I opened the hatch, this white couple's jaws just dropped.

They obviously didn't expect to see me and two mixed-race kids inside.

So, of course, the litany of questions started: *Where do you live? What do you do?*

I didn't want to tell them what I did, so I said that I'm a car collector and rattled off a few of my cars. The man pointed at the Sherp. "What is *this* called?"

I told him and he immediately pulled out his phone. I just knew he was looking up how much it cost.

I braced myself for what I knew was coming next. The guys at Home Depot—whether inside or in the parking lot—see me and want to say, "Wait, how come you have that?" This obviously well-off white couple who only dealt with people who looked like them would never say that to me, and they probably liked to think of themselves as without prejudice, but they were about to say something that was equally damning: "Good for you."

Ninety percent of my conversations with people like this end with this phrase. I'm sure they think they mean well, but whenever someone looks at me, nods, and says, "Good for you," it feels wrong. Because what they're really saying is, *It's good to see Black people doing something good for a change.*

Good for you.

Arghhhhh.

I sometimes think about working up the nerve to ask someone what they mean by "Good for you." But that's something an Angry Black Man would ask, and that's not who I am.

And it probably wouldn't end well for us.

I'd never bring any of this up on the channel. After all, I try to tread lightly on race on *Rich Rebuilds*, because it could turn into something super dark very fast. The last thing I want is to scare people away from the channel, because cancel culture has become such a big thing. And I know my audience: 98 percent white people between the ages of twenty-five and fifty-six. I'm not in a position to lose them just yet.

Good for you.

Sometimes when I hear that, I think, *Now I understand. You've never seen a successful Black person around these parts before.*

And I can't get mad because, to tell you the truth, neither have I.

On the flip side, once the channel began to get serious traction, it wasn't long before I started to receive backlash from people in the African American community asking why I didn't have more Black people in my videos. I've read threads on online forums where the complaints go on and on. *What's Uncle Rich doing for the people? All I see in his videos are white people. What message is he sending us? He's lost his roots.*

It even happens with comments on my own videos. In fact, for at least a year or two, there was one viewer who left the same comment each week without fail: "How come there are no Black people in your videos?"

I'll admit, it's a real conundrum. I live in Salem, Massachusetts, where 7 percent of the population is Black, which is better than Seabrook, New Hampshire—where we launched the first Electrified Garage—which has an African American population of 0.5 percent. The population literally changes two points when I cross over the New Hampshire border.

I don't intentionally surround myself with people who are white. They just happen to be people who live near me, are comfortable on camera, and can deal with my warped sense of humor. That's a tall order all by itself. Finding African American men and women who want to be in my videos and can knowledgeably riff about and work on unusual cars—punctuated with the sarcasm that underscores every video—has been close to impossible. I asked one of my Black friends who's into cars to do a video with me, but he turned me down because he's not into my humor.

One day, I came up with a partial solution. As some viewers have noticed, I can be viciously sarcastic, though I tend to regard it as a defense mechanism: if I'm not serious about something and I don't show my emotions, then another person can't hurt me.

But in this age of social media, once you let people know how to push your buttons, they'll never stop. So I've thought about answering my critics with an honest plan: I'll hire a group of professional African American actors to appear in one episode. And I'll directly address the camera and say, "Hey, listen up. You guys have been saying that I haven't had any Black people on the channel. So here you go. Here's fifteen of them."

Then we'll all do Black people things, like go for walks, have dinner, and talk about sports.

In reality, since I've been on the hunt, I've collaborated with many Black YouTubers: Demonology (a twenty-hour drive away), Megan's Welder (thirty-seven hours), DoctaM3 (nine hours), and Mod2Fame (five hours). You may find it strange that I'm listing these names, but I'm doing this so I can refer people who doubt my diversity efforts to this page. If you are reading this and are Asian, please contact me.

I've noticed a weird righteousness with a lot of white people. It's actually kind of adorable, because they want to stick up for people of color, but they frequently end up making a big deal out of something that probably isn't.

One day, I went out to lunch with a bunch of friends, and we all paid separately with cash. One friend noticed that the cashier put their change directly into their hand, but when I paid my bill, the cashier threw the change on the counter.

"It's because you're Black," said my friend, all pumped up for a fight. But my mind doesn't immediately go there. It could very well be the reason, but it could also just be an honest mistake. I always try to give people the benefit of the doubt, because if I *do* go there and think about why certain things only happen to me, it'll just add to the long list of things that already keep me up at night, and I'd never leave the house. Bring on the brownies.

Even when I'm at home, I can't escape it. When we first bought our house in a development of new houses in Salem, I was puttering in the yard when an older woman walked by with her dog. She waved and said, "Oh, what a beautiful home."

"Yes it is," I said, wanting to be friendly with my new neighbor.

"Are the owners home?" she asked.

Like I said, I try not to go there, but sometimes it's right there in my face. In most cases, it wouldn't accomplish anything to be antagonistic, and besides, like I've said, I consider it my duty to teach people something new whenever possible. So I shrugged and said, "They'll be home later."

Sometimes you just have to take it in stride. Ironically, it wasn't until I seriously got into cars that race became a real and present issue.

Years ago, I registered for a car show over the phone, and they asked the usual slate of questions: name, address, phone number.

All good. Then, "What's your race?"

My race? What does that matter? I just want to go to a car show and have a good time. I know it's for marketing and demographic purposes, but these metrics get forced down your throat and you're constantly reminded that you're different from everyone else. And it's not just Black people but Asians and Latinos too—you name it.

As much as we want to ignore race, it permeates every single aspect of American life. When you turn on the TV, read the newspaper, or go online, the issue of race is there at every turn. It's impossible to avoid. People think it's not worth talking about, but most people don't have the skills necessary to navigate these types of conversations constructively. I personally believe part of my success is due to the fact that I am Black. It's a difficult concept to understand, but let's face it: a person with a white skin tone is the norm on YouTube, and everything else is a deviation.

Sometimes, it's pretty funny. One day I was driving around with my buddy in my Corvette. We were at a stoplight, and a homeless guy ran up to the passenger side and started talking to my friend, who's white. The guy said, "Awesome car, man. Can you spare a buck?" Then he looked over at me and literally screamed, "Holy shit! A Black guy owns this!" I busted out laughing and gave him two dollars.

But usually, it's just depressing. A viewer once sent me a thoughtful, detailed email.

"Hey man, love the channel. I know sometimes it's hard and you want to quit, but keep it up because there are a lot of people rooting for you."

Nice opening line. But I didn't relax. I *never* relax, because I always know what's coming next.

"But just remember that you're black…"

Did he think I had forgotten?

"…and that's never going to change. You'll always be ten steps behind the white man because after all our brains are 3% larger and we're much more superior than you."

And so on for several more paragraphs.

I always refer back to what my father told me: that people are going to look at me differently because I don't look like them. Then there's the added complication that a lot of people don't know what to make of me, because I don't neatly fit into their idea of what a Black man should be. Some variation of this happens every day of my life, but it also helps justify my philosophy: I have to be nice to everyone because I don't know whose mind I'll be able to change. So it's up to me to break that mold and give them what they least expect.

After I finished reading that email, I thought, *Alright, watch this.*

I wrote him back and said, "Thanks for the email. Don't forget to like, share, and subscribe."

One day, I'd like to not constantly be reminded that I'm different.

But I'm not holding my breath.

A RAISIN IN THE OATMEAL

Recently a new car repair shop opened up in Gloucester, the next town over from Salem. They threw a party to celebrate, and I was invited. There were about thirty people there, all white. I was the lone raisin in the oatmeal. Some of the people there may have heard of me, but I assumed that most hadn't.

I was talking with a guy in his thirties who was telling me about his BMW. I told him I had the same model and proceeded to rattle off the modifications I'd made to it.

After a few minutes, he looked confused and excused himself. Maybe he thought I only did EV stuff? But a few days later, a friend told me that the guy had talked to him about me, saying that he had never talked to a Black person before, and he had no idea that we could be that articulate.

When my friend told me this, I almost got upset. But I pushed it away because, odds are, this person was probably right. Gloucester's about 91 percent white compared to Salem's 80 percent, and I will say that my city's diversity is a big reason why my wife and I decided to raise our kids here. In other words, if you were born and raised in Gloucester, Massachusetts, you might see one or two Black kids at Gloucester High School, possibly none.

My friend also told me that the shop owner told him, "I don't want that nigger back in my shop."

Like I said, I have to shrug it off, or else I'd never get out of bed in the morning.

HEY, RICH, WAS THAT YOU?

In the early days, when the channel first started to take off, I often got texts and calls from friends who were mad at me because they thought they saw me drive by in my Tesla in Vegas or Los Angeles and I didn't tell them I was in town.

Today, I don't get as many calls or texts about a case of mistaken identity, because apparently there are a lot more Black people who drive Teslas. But as with everything else, I've learned not to let it get to me. I have to let it roll off my shoulders, whether it's on YouTube or in real life. And I won't lie, sometimes it's actually kind of fun.

But in general, people are just strange.

CHAPTER ELEVEN

ICE-T

The truth is, I'm just one big ball of nostalgia. I always want to be reminded of how far I've come.

Which means that I often prefer old stuff to the latest and greatest in technological advances. Besides, compared with electric vehicles, gas-powered cars engage all five senses.

The initial bark that a car makes when it's been sitting overnight—or longer—is one of my favorite sounds in the world. When you start a car that's been sitting for more than a few hours, the starter has to kick over to make the engine crank, and all the metal starts pinging because when heat is applied to metal, it expands.

Every make and model of car sounds different, which gives each vehicle its own unique personality. If you start any one of my cars up, I can tell you which one it is with my eyes closed. Of course, high-end sports cars have their own distinctive tone, and the manufacturers tune them on purpose to give drivers a certain emotional connection to the car. Porsche tunes their exhausts to a particular note, and so do Ferrari and Lamborghini.

While I love to hear that cold-start pinging and the roar of an exhaust, I love distinctive car smells even more, whether it's the leather interior in a new or new-to-me car or the exhaust from an old muscle car the first time it's started up after a long winter.

But I especially love the smell of gasoline. To be honest, I'm amazed I don't have brain damage from all the fumes I've inhaled.

All these smells conjure up a kind of fuzzy nostalgia from when I was a kid and first fell in love with cars. Specifically, the first car I ever loved: my mom's base-model, periwinkle-blue Geo Prizm. She told me that the car would be mine when I turned sixteen, so I took meticulous care of it. In addition to sneaking it out of the driveway, I was always cleaning it, with KRS-One, LL Cool J, and Ice Cube blasting from the stereo while the guys in the neighborhood who drove around in a high-end Lexus chuckled. Little did they know, one day I'd be washing my own Porsche.

The Geo was the worst brand out there, an absolute tin-can econobox. But once my mother let me use it, I became responsible for everything, including filling the gas tank. The first time the needle hit *E*, I drove to the gas station around the corner and put the nozzle into the car.

I had never put gas in a car before, and when I squeezed the nozzle, nothing happened. So I pulled it out and squeezed it again. This time gas poured onto the ground, and an angry guy came running out of the station to yell at me.

It's an important memory for me because it represents the first car I ever owned. And every time I fill up a car, I'm brought back to that day and how important it was—and still is—to me.

Today, Chad will rag on me because, even with a fully equipped shop, I'll still reach for a hand tool over a power tool. Just as the sounds of a cold-start engine bring me back to an earlier, simpler time, it all comes down to nostalgia. When I first started working on cars, I couldn't afford any power tools, so I worked with hand tools instead. I had no choice.

I particularly love ratcheting wrenches because they provide me with instant feedback: I can actually hear each individual click, so I know when it's loosening and when it's tightening because there's a different sound to each. Plus, it's just more satisfying to wrench something by hand instead of using a battery-powered ratchet that stops automatically. Power tools are too predictable; I know exactly what's going to happen with each click. I prefer to work by the seat of my pants when it comes to making a video, and the same applies to working on cars, particularly old cars.

My preference for hand tools also means that working on a pre-1990s carbureted car is a lot more satisfying. I spend the vast majority of my waking hours either on my phone or listening to it constantly ping, so any time I can do something that doesn't require another screen or computer, I'm happy. Older cars are so simple. Even better, everything you do is your own fault, and you never have to question if one of the computer components needs an update or there's a bug in the system.

On an old car, once you've checked that all the mechanical parts are solid, if something isn't working, you probably didn't tighten the battery terminal down or inject the carburetor correctly. Sure, there are a lot more moving pieces in an old car, but it's easy to figure things out by trial and error.

In fact, while I loved working on the i8 hybrid, once it was done I wasn't crazy about it because it has computerized exhaust notes. These work in two different ways: First, a computer pumps fake exhaust noises into the cabin. Second, what looks like an exhaust pipe is actually a subwoofer. So when you drive, the car plays fake exhaust notes both inside and outside the car. There's also a microphone in the engine compartment that replicates the noises and plays them back in the cabin.

When I first drove the i8, I honestly thought the sounds were coming from the car, but once I realized what was going on, it felt like I was being bamboozled. BMW has no choice, because most people who make the transition from gas to electric can't let go of that kind of feedback from the engine. The i8 is powered by a basic, run-of-the-mill three-cylinder engine out of a Mini Cooper, which never sounds good. So BMW—and other car manufacturers—has to replicate better engine sounds by pumping in fake noises. Of course, it's where car manufacturers are headed, but I'm not a huge fan.

Maybe I'm just a Luddite at heart, because I like working on cars the hard way: on the ground, creeping under a car on my back, using my ratcheting wrenches. That's the way I've always done things. I have multiple lifts in my shop, and I'm still not used to the idea of using them.

Of course, Chris and Chad and the other guys rib me about this. They say that they'll help me, and while it's great that I have the help, I would much rather work alone at my own pace.

I was starting to cast around for my next project after the RS7.

I looked around at the cars in my yard and at the shop. There was yet another salvaged Tesla that had been underwater. It needed a motor, a battery, and all the internal electronics.

At this point, I was bored to tears with working on Teslas—and of course, I didn't want to get the Musk hive buzzing again—so I started to brainstorm. So far, I'd switched batteries, changed motors, and added more power to Teslas. What could I do with one that hadn't already been done that wouldn't require me to go to Tesla—since, of course, they were not going to sell me a single part?

The next logical question was *Who will sell me parts?* Only everyone else. And which manufacturer have I been working with since I first started working on cars? General Motors.

The light bulb switched on.

What if I turned the Tesla into a gas-powered car?

It was a crazy idea, more tongue-in-cheek to underscore how ludicrous Tesla's policies were, but the more I thought about it, the more I needed to do it to prove a point. If Tesla won't help me fix this car, then I'll find someone who will.

That's how I came up with the idea for the V8 Tesla, which was named ICE-T, short for Internal Combustion Engine Tesla.

Converting a car from gas to electric is very easy. The basic components are simple: after you remove the engine, you put in a battery, a motor, and a controller that tells the battery how much power to give the motor.

But going from electric to gas is extraordinarily difficult, because there are more and larger components that have to fit into a smaller space. An internal combustion engine is massive. Where are you going to put it? Then, where do the fuel tank and fuel pump go, and how do you route the exhaust system in order to get rid of the poisonous gases? These are daunting tasks and more than most skilled mechanics would ever want to deal with. But wait, there's more! You then have to figure out how to integrate the systems together.

It was definitely not for the faint of heart, and I had serious doubts about whether I could pull it off. But it *was* different. And more importantly, no one else had attempted it.

That was enough for me.

Even though my mantra has always been *I can do that*, I know when a project is more than I can handle solo. Dolores, the RS7, and the i8 were all projects that I felt comfortable doing on my own, though of course I did have people helping me along the way.

ICE-T was the first big project that I knew I couldn't handle by myself, because it required *everything*: welding, fabrication, master mechanics who knew how to fit square pegs in round holes, and then some. It was a true collective: The Electrified Garage in Florida built the engine. Joshua Dodge in Winchendon, Massachusetts, did all the fabrication work, from cutting the car in half to welding the transmission tunnel. Chad handled all the electrical wiring. I had a very clear picture of what I wanted the end result to be, and I could have built ICE-T myself, but I knew if I did it alone I'd still be working on it five years later, and that was never in the cards. It was by far my longest project. ICE-T took two years, from start to finish.

When it was all over, ICE-T also served as one big middle finger to all the doubters who said it couldn't be done.

After I finish a build, I usually want to be the first to drive the car. When I built Dolores, I had to be the first person to drive her because it was such an earth-shattering moment for me. I had a GoPro behind my head and I was recording everything myself. I also wanted to be the first one to drive the RS7 and the i8 when those projects were completed.

But as I finished later projects, it almost felt like having a second child. Okay, guys, I get it. I'm not saying that these cars aren't special, but it's like, okay, I've been through this before. Welcome to the world.

With ICE-T, because it was such a collaborative effort, I let the guys take the first drives. Besides, I could guarantee that they would be much more excited than I would be to drive the car for the first time.

As I watched Chad and Joshua take the car out for a spin, I was telling all the doubters and detractors through the years: Look at me. Look at what I can do.

It was the best feeling in the world.

BEING A MASSHOLE

The reason I'm still in Massachusetts is that I was born and raised here, though I never wanted to live in a cold climate, and I don't understand people who enjoy doing cold-weather sports. My kids take ski lessons, and while I think it's a very cool thing to know how to do, I'll just stay in the car, thanks.

I don't like when I can't do something because of the temperature. Sometimes I want to work on a car and drive like a maniac on a Sunday morning. But I can't do those things, because: winter. The cold and I don't get along very well. I'd love it if I could be warm all the time.

I'd love to move to New Hampshire so I could have more land for my cars, but then again, *winter*. I'm not a big fan of Massachusetts. I'm just used to it because I grew up here, but I would love to live someplace else, maybe the Carolinas. Though, so far, my favorite places to visit have been Arizona and Austin, which is like a mini Boston with all the young people, except the weather's beautiful. I would pretty much enjoy living anywhere else, and if I could move my whole family unit from this state to another one, I'd do it.

But it's probably not going to happen anytime soon, if it ever does. Besides, I just have too much crap to move. So I try not to think about it much, and instead I just travel as much as I can. That way, I can get a taste of everywhere and not really commit to anything.

Which of course has been the story of my life.

U-DRIVE-IT

I have friends who own Teslas who launch into full self-driving mode the second they back out of their driveway.

I hate that. As a society, we've gotten so lazy. Everyone keeps bragging about full self-driving, but I love to drive, maybe too much. After all, I waited the first fifteen years of my life to drive. Why would I want the car to drive for me?

Whenever I think of full self-driving, I think of myself as a young boy. I remember that I wanted to drive a car so badly, when I finally turned fifteen and could get my learner's permit, I was jumping out of my skin. I was so excited.

I wanted nothing more in life than to drive a car. I was so inspired by engines and transmissions and exhaust sounds. That's why I'm so passionate about cars today. Imagine working your way up in life just to have the car drive you . . . I just can't do it.

Sure, there are long stretches of empty road that are kind of boring or times when I want to use the phone. Then I think it's fine to let the car take over.

But the idea that a car can drive me anywhere and everywhere? The little boy in me is just screaming: *What the hell are you doing? You've wanted this for so long and now it's doing it for you?* I couldn't live like that.

CHAPTER TWELVE

UNSOCIAL MEDIA

Admittedly, it was hard to follow ICE-T.

Partly because, how could I ever top that project? But also because YouTube—and social media overall—was becoming increasingly competitive. It looked so easy—and financially rewarding—that everyone wanted in.

Ten years ago, if you asked a kid what they wanted to be when they grew up, the top answers among boys were doctor, lawyer, firefighter, or baseball player. Girls would answer teacher, ballerina, veterinarian, or doctor.

Today, the number one answer among both boys and girls is social media influencer. This shouldn't be a surprise, because that's all they see. If you have a phone—and these days, what kid doesn't?—you're already halfway there: stick it in your face, start talking, and the bucks will start rolling in, or so everybody thinks. After all, it looks so easy.

Wander around online and you'll see some five-year-old who's pulling in $30 million a year reviewing toys on YouTube. His parents are there, off in the periphery, filming almost every second of his childhood with an iPhone.

When I first started the channel and told people I was on YouTube, they'd often say, "I don't know how you make money. You must be a struggling artist." Today, their eyes light up. "Ohhhh, you must be making lots of that YouTube money."

The automotive field—even within very narrow niches— has gotten extremely crowded with new influencers who are very hungry. They want to grab as much market share as they can right out of the starting gate, so instead of posting a new video once a week, they're posting every day or more. More videos are competing for the same limited number of eyeballs, so viewership has been dropping across the board. After all, there are only so many hours in a day, and many of my peers from my early days have faded. In some cases, they've quit altogether.

When *Game of Thrones* first came out, it was iconic. There was only one show like it and everyone had heard of it, even if they didn't watch. Now, there are ten shows like it and no one knows their names.

The same goes for the YouTube car space. In the automotive sector alone, there are countless genres to specialize in: pickup trucks, sports cars, brands like Volkswagen and Porsche, vintage vehicles.

Everyone on social media is trying to outdo each other. At one point, the trend was to do good deeds, all in the name of bumping up the numbers. First it was "Hey, I bought my mom a car." Then it was "Hey, I bought my dad a house." Recently, I saw someone say, "Hey, I bought this homeless guy teeth." Everyone's spending a lot of money just to one-up each other. Tavarish, one of my YouTube colleagues, just purchased a car for well north of $500,000, which blows my mind. While he obviously loved the car, he felt that he had to spend the money to stay ahead of the competition.

Competition is a tough word, because even though I think everyone in the YouTube automotive and comedy space is a potential competitor, I still believe that there's room for all of us.

For me, the real issue is time. There's never enough to do everything I want to do, even with people helping me out in the shop and with editing the videos. Viewers have come to expect a new twenty- to thirty-minute video each week as an absolute minimum, and producing that much content is a grueling and unforgiving process that chews up time. There's always something that ends up on the cutting-room floor because I'm bumping up against the deadline.

In 2023, I made the radical decision to stop releasing a new video every weekend.

Putting out a video every week was probably the most stressful thing I've ever done in my life because it made me feel like I constantly had a gun pointed at the back of my head. I always felt like I had to be doing something for future videos, whether contacting prospective sponsors, working on a build, planning the next build, shooting the video, editing the video, or planning the video for the following week.

Instead of doing things that I enjoyed, I became a slave to the work, and I always felt extreme pressure to create just to get something out there. Since I had to start working on the following week's video the week before, at any given point in time I was working on two videos at once, and usually more if I was in the middle of a series. I got backed up and started to release content that I didn't feel was my best work.

I didn't like doing what I was doing, and my viewers also became confused. They started to ask, "What's this stuff he's putting out? It doesn't really seem like something Rich would do." When I didn't have a video planned, I would literally go out and buy something just so I could film it. Once I bought a miniature bulldozer. I wasn't even making it electric because there wasn't enough time. I had to do the build in five days, which was insane. I had to fix it up, paint it, and add lighting. It was weird and quirky, and I wasn't that excited about it. Viewers didn't think much of it either, because who really wants to see a mini bulldozer? I ended up wasting thousands of dollars on something that didn't make any sense. What *did* make sense was to skip that week so I could dedicate more time to other long-term projects and produce a better video.

It didn't take long to feel like I was back working for someone else, with a boss who was telling me that I had to do what he wanted me to do. That was why I'd quit my last job, because I didn't want to do that anymore.

I felt like I was answering to the needs of other people, not to myself. Even though the money was great, I realized that my quality of life was far more important. I will happily take a reduction in pay as long as I get to live the life that I want to live. So after being in this cycle for a while, I finally decided that I wasn't going to release a video every Sunday anymore. Instead, I'd release a video when *I* felt it was right, when everything was in place. Now, I have control over my life again, and it's an absolutely amazing feeling.

I've gotten some backlash, since viewers had gotten used to seeing a new video every Sunday, but many people told me they'd rather I take my time to put out something that I'm proud of instead of just spitting out content for the sake of content.

And now I have my weekends back.

There's a skit from *30 Rock* where Steve Buscemi plays an old man who goes undercover as a student at a local high school and is painfully out of touch. He's wearing a backward cap and has a backpack and a skateboard, and he asks, "How do you do, fellow kids?" in the hallway.

If there's a situation where I can look, feel, or act younger, I'll do it, because I like living in the mindset of a kid. But I'm always checking myself to make sure I don't come across as an old guy trying to act young, even though most people think I'm a lot younger than I am. I'm in really good shape, and as the saying goes, "Black don't crack." Most people think I'm lying when I say I have three kids, and one is in her twenties.

But today, everything makes me feel old, and getting old is scary. I'm in my forties and worry about not being relevant anymore, since, after all, youth is the moneymaker in the YouTube social hierarchy. If you're in your twenties, you're hip, and if you're in your thirties or forties, you're in a different class that's not as appealing or financially lucrative. It's a real challenge. After all, if people think I'm old and not cool anymore, I won't make money, and then what happens? As a result, staying relevant is a huge deal for me.

I think I'm so attached to acting and feeling young because I missed out on a lot of my youth when I became a father at the age of eighteen. Having my daughter was an absolute blessing, but I sacrificed a lot of years when I was forced to grow up at a young age. We listen to the same music and go to concerts together. But one of my greatest fears is: *What if my daughter doesn't want to hang out with me anymore?* So I try to stay young because I want her to think I'm cool and interesting.

My son quizzes me about new popular memes, and I try to watch a lot of TikTok. I think it's very difficult to entertain someone in twenty seconds, and watching people doing stupid things gives me a great bit of joy. I like very quick entertainment, since that's all that my ADHD can handle. I can go through fifteen or twenty funny videos in fifteen minutes and get my fill from that.

I've decided that the best way to set myself apart on YouTube is just to keep doing what I've been doing: picking a quirky build that no one's done before and making videos about the challenges and surprises I encounter along the way.

In fact, I've discovered that when I stray from straight-forward car-build videos, the number of viewers increases exponentially. For instance, the videos about taking my one-millionth subscriber's wife out to dinner, buying a Porsche for my girlfriend of two weeks, and stealing my Tinder date's car all pulled in significantly more viewers than the vast major-ity of build-focused videos, and in a much shorter period of time.

I find this mind-blowing because, compared to the cost of the builds, these softer videos basically cost nothing. With the two-week girlfriend video, I bought her dinner and we called it even. And yet that video outperformed others featuring cars that cost almost six figures.

They also take a lot less time to produce, since I don't have to spend hours puzzling out a problem to get one minute of video. They also cater to viewers and subscribers who are really curious to know more about my private life.

However, there is one big caveat. If someone who's new to the channel watches one of these softer videos before he sees a straightforward build video, there's a good chance he'll assume that the rest of the videos on the channel are similar. If he didn't like the softer video—either he thought he was going to get more car in the video or he thought I was a jerk—then he may never watch another video. In fact, when I watch these softer videos, I sometimes think that if I didn't know this per-son, I would think he's a jerk too.

With that said, I'm considering creating more of them in the future because they have brought up an important point: maybe it's possible to rely more on my personality instead of buying a bunch of expensive cars, which can consume weeks of my time and only produce a couple of videos. It's certainly started me thinking about switching things up and sprinkling more of these lighter videos into the mix.

Besides, it will satisfy those viewers who are curious about my real life, even if I intentionally paint a totally inaccurate depiction of it.

After all, my viewership—and the kinds of videos I post—has certainly changed over the years. When I first started posting on YouTube, most viewers tuned in because they wanted to learn about Teslas. Today, they're more interested in being entertained than in learning something new, which is probably a side effect of this ultracompetitive trend where everyone is practically required to do more expensive, whiz-bang builds just to avoid losing market share.

After all, how many more cars can you watch being rebuilt? How many more front bumpers can you watch someone put on? If you type in any car, any make and model, even a Ferrari Dino, I guarantee you there are hundreds of videos showing it being taken apart and put back together every which way.

How do you stay relevant? How do you stay at the top of people's minds when your marketplace is getting saturated? For me, I've decided that my personality will help: those are my jokes and that's my humor. Believe it or not, it's very rare to find a sense of humor in the car space, so that definitely helps me to stand out. The softer videos allow me to show more of my humor than the straightforward car features.

Sure, there are plenty of videos that show a bunch of guys standing around in a garage, talking and laughing while they're wrenching on cars. Of course, there's been plenty of that on the channel, but I do a lot more than just fix cars. *Rich Rebuilds* is more like a regular TV show, with new episodes appearing regularly. And to be honest, I've always tried to make my videos funny and a little cheeky, even back when I only had a hundred subscribers.

In "Rich Gets His Reward?," which I posted on February 20, 2018, my wife wanted me to fix a busted door handle on her car and swap out the snow tires. She told me that if I got everything done by Saturday night, then we could have sex. The video showed me running around in fast motion doing it all. Toward the end of the video, I headed upstairs and into the bedroom, only to find Allison fast asleep in bed, covers pulled up over her head.

With that video, I wanted to put my foot on the ground to establish the tone and humor going forward, to say, "Hey, this is who I am and this is what you can expect from the channel."

People care about the car stuff, but not really. After all, there are many, many comments that essentially say, "Thanks for making me laugh. I'd be happy just watching you playing with Legos."

Me too, buddy, me too.

Since I was a latchkey kid, I spent a good chunk of my childhood by myself. Once I entered high school, however, I was pretty much surrounded by people for most of my waking hours, and that soon became my norm.

Once *Rich Rebuilds* took off and I was in the spotlight, time alone became a very rare commodity. Somebody always wanted something from me or needed an answer *that day*, and there was always another email to send or phone call to return. Because of that, I started to crave alone time again. To counteract the nonstop onslaught, sometimes I just want to lay low and not talk to anyone for a very long time.

I never really realized the power of solitude, and I quickly learned that the only way for me to tune it all out is to be by myself. Since professional mechanics are used to being on the clock, they're accustomed to cranking away as fast as possible. When I'm working on a car and no one's around, I can work at my own pace and take breaks whenever I want.

Other times, when I want to be by myself, I'll sit in a room alone with my own thoughts and write down whatever pops into my mind.

It took me some time to get used to being alone, but I've learned that there's great power and peace that comes when I spend time with myself.

SHERP ON ICE . . . AND OTHER MISADVENTURES

One day, I got a text from a guy in New Hampshire who asked if I wanted to go ice fishing in the Sherp.

Not too long after that, another guy from New Hampshire—seriously, what's in the water up there?—asked if I'd like to put my recently acquired farm truck through its paces by helping him with haying.

When I was a kid, there wasn't even an imaginary world that included either farming or stepping onto a frozen lake, but since starting the channel I've had countless experiences that I never would've had. Experiencing these things for the first time is really groundbreaking.

A week after the invitation to go ice fishing, I was out in the middle of Lake Winnipesaukee on a zero-degree day in the Sherp, crawling across the ice and churning through open water. To be honest, even walking across ice scares me to death, and a million questions immediately float up: *How thick is the ice? How cold is the water? What giant creatures are lurking just under the surface hoping to grab my foot?* But in the endless quest for great video, out I went. Within minutes, the Sherp had broken through the ice and was churning through frigid water, and at one point it was almost nose down in the lake. If that Sherp took on too much water, I would've straight up died.

I admit I've taken a lot of stupid chances through the years, but I've never been that terrified. Thankfully, the Sherp made it back onto the ice, but for the rest of the day I couldn't stop shaking, and it wasn't just because of the cold.

My farm adventure was the exact opposite in terms of temperature and danger. I'd never worked on a farm before, and it was ungodly hot that day—ninety degrees in the shade—but at least the truck was put through its paces. Of course, I made lots of mistakes, which generated some good video, and the farmer got his hay in from the fields with free labor.

In both instances, because the activities were new to me, I almost felt like a child seeing Santa Claus for the first time, and I got to bring an audience along for the journey.

Like the rest of my videos, these on-location shoots are never planned. Instead, it's *Hey, this seems like a good idea. Let's try this.*

So if you have a good idea for an on-location shoot, I'm all ears.

NINE LIVES AND COUNTING

Chris likes to say that I'm a cat, and that I probably used up most of my nine lives working on Dolores.

In some of the early videos, a lot of people thought I was taking crazy risks, which probably boosted viewership. Of course, there are always safety protocols to follow, but tasks like testing the batteries and disconnecting a high-voltage loop beforehand don't always make for scintillating video. And sometimes I didn't wear gloves, either because the camera angle was all wrong or because I couldn't hold the phone to shoot with the gloves on.

And I didn't have time to go back and film footage showing me testing the batteries.

A few years back, I probably used up at least one life, maybe two, when I drove to Canada to pick up a car. I have a Toyota Tacoma V6, which has a seven-thousand-pound towing capacity. I had gotten the car and was heading home, going at least seventy or eighty kilometers per hour and listening to a song on the radio that had a really good vibe. I was driving along and nodding my head with the beat when I thought, "Wow, this song has a lot more bass than I remember."

I turned the radio down and heard a giant thumping noise followed by the loudest explosion I've ever heard in my life. All of a sudden, the car I was towing started to fishtail all over the road and I lost control of the truck. I managed to pull into a ditch, where I opened the door at the exact moment that the wheel of my truck slammed into the back of my leg. It must have fallen off a ways back but kept rolling until I stepped out to assess the damage.

It was by far the most intense pain I'd ever felt in my life. But I'm pretty weird: whenever I'm in the middle of a traumatic event, I always try to look at the good side. So even while I was in extreme pain, I told myself, *Rich, I know this is painful, but at least you didn't lose the wheel.*

Better yet, next time, have the wheel hit someone else.

CHAPTER THIRTEEN

EVERYTHING YOU EVER WANTED TO KNOW ABOUT LEENDA BUT WERE AFRAID TO ASK

When I first started the channel, I thought I knew how viewers were going to react whenever I posted a new video—what they would like most about the video and what they'd complain about.

I had to throw that out the window, because the truth is that it's impossible to predict what will make people go absolutely nuts and send views into the stratosphere, and what they're going to hate and make them unsubscribe.

But nothing surprised me more than when I decided to add a new female character to the show named Leenda.

I'd wanted to add a female assistant to the channel for a while, since I thought it would breathe new life into the show. It's the same with any long-running TV program: the show starts out great, but after some time it starts to feel a bit stale or another show comes along that cuts into viewership.

My audience is 98 percent male, and car culture has featured scantily clad women draped across the hoods of countless automobiles since the first Model A Ford rolled off the line. But I'd never seen any electric car company or conversion company feature a female model alongside their cars, so it was something I had been pondering for a while, because I knew it would provide me with another way to stand apart.

You'll have to forgive me here for making the following blanket statement, but it's been my experience that guys who are into electric vehicle conversions don't tend to be ladies' men. In fact, many tend to be nerds who spend a lot of time in front of their computers or in their basements.

There, I said it.

Of course, I speak from personal experience.

The hard truth about YouTube is that viewers often decide to watch a new video based on the thumbnail photo on the home page. Carl and I often played around with suggestive words to superimpose on the picture, like "HAMMER TIME" and

"BIG MOTOR, SMALL HOLE," but I knew that a photo could also make a huge difference. I decided to experiment with the first video featuring the Mini Cooper: "We Built an Electric Mini Cooper for Under $3,000 and It's Awesome!" In the thumbnail for that video, I was holding my puppy Biscuit, and almost immediately the video pulled in way more views than the previous episode.

If a dog could boost viewership, what could an attractive woman do?

I went on Craigslist and posted a notice looking for a female assistant, with the requirement that the successful applicant had to know something about cars—or at least be comfortable around them—and know the difference between an oil filter and an air filter. I quickly learned that searching for a qualified actress on Craigslist wasn't the best place, because I mostly heard from sex workers and women who were clearly unstable.

One day, a model and actress by the name of Leenda Lucia showed up, and when we shot the first video, I knew she was a great fit. For one, she frequently modeled at car shows on the East Coast, so she was comfortable around cars—and the men who loved them—and she also had a take-no-prisoners attitude that would stand up to our male-dominated, snarky, occasionally suggestive sense of humor on the channel.

Leenda made her first appearance in the video "Should I Replace My Audi RS7 with This Cheap Mercedes AMG?" and viewership doubled almost immediately.

I wasn't sure what to think. On the one hand, the majority of the comments were now about Leenda, not my stellar skills and sense of humor. On the other hand, she had significantly boosted viewership—and therefore my income—in a matter of weeks. I posted a link to her Instagram page, so many viewers checked out her social media as well. We had shot enough footage of her in one day to slot into several videos, and whenever Leenda appeared in the thumbnail, the same thing happened: there was a big boost in viewers and subscribers. I never imagined that bringing on a female assistant would be this successful.

There was something else that I didn't expect. I've always known that fans have been very curious about my life off camera, but bringing Leenda on board created a *lot* of chatter, sometimes too much.

Viewers have always made up very detailed stories about my life in the Comments, endlessly speculating as to whether I'm married or divorced, but when Leenda started appearing in videos, the speculation increased exponentially. For the first couple of years of the channel, if you googled *Rich Rebuilds*, "Tesla" was always the first auto-complete result based on users' searches. But once Leenda showed up, "Tesla" didn't even appear in the top five anymore. Instead, it was "wife," "assistant," "Leenda," "divorce," and "net worth."

I suppose it's natural for people to want to know more about someone they watch every week or so and what my life is like off camera, from what my house looks like to the cars I drive. I admit that I enjoy intentionally confusing people because, quite frankly, it's no one's business. But I decided to not address the speculation, especially after Leenda became a recurring character. After all, one reason I think the videos do so well is because they create a mystery. It's like I'm dropping a bunch of hints but not providing any answers.

In the Comments section, some viewers admitted that they didn't care what I was talking about, they just wanted to see Leenda again. Some YouTubers I know would take issue with that, but I considered it to be a big success. If people are watching the video, they're still learning about cars, because that's been my goal all along: to teach people in such a way that they're learning and don't even know it. Later, at a party, they'll be able to honestly tell someone how an electric motor works.

Now I'm going to turn it over to Leenda.

#LeendaLucia

When I first met Rich, I'd been working in the car industry for several years as a freelance model. Since I'm not six feet tall and a size two, I had to create my own opportunities because no modeling agency would touch me. Modeling for car shows and at corporate events was the only way I could launch and then grow my career.

When I showed up for the first video, I thought it was just a modeling gig. I figured we'd take a few photos with some different cars and then shoot some video for a couple of segments, so I brought a bunch of outfits.

We created a narrative revolving around me being his assistant, that I'm a little bit spacey, and that I only care about social media and taking selfies.

The shoot was pretty straightforward. Nothing was rehearsed and nothing was staged. We all improvised, and it was very fast-paced and smart. I quickly discovered that Rich is supersmart but also extremely sarcastic, and that I had to be witty and sharp to keep up with him. We instantly clicked and spent most of the shoot bantering and bickering back and forth. It didn't feel like we were working at all.

When we wrapped up the shoot, I felt like I had known Rich forever.

When I left, I thought, *This is how you make a career?* I thought it was hilarious.

Based on viewer comments—and the boost in subscriber numbers—it was obvious that Rich wanted me back. The formula didn't change: in every video he cranks on some random car and tells me what I need to do.

We improvise the whole time, and nothing is ever written down. I bring nicer clothes for the thumbnail still photos and then crappy clothes, because it didn't take me long to find out that he's probably going to have me crawling under a greasy hood or pushing something through the freaking mud.

It's all fun and games, but it's important that the storyline stays consistent, so once we start shooting we figure out my entrance and exit from the video to continue the storyline from my last appearance. For instance, in one video in the summer of 2022, we worked on a farm in New Hampshire, helping a farmer cut and bale hay. It was ninety degrees most of the day, and it was incredibly hard work. At the end of the video, Rich paid me just a dollar. I said, "What the hell is this?" and stormed off. My next appearance was in the "Building a Better Electric Motorcycle than Harley Davidson" video, and I just randomly showed up one day at the beginning of the video and Rich said he hadn't seen me since I'd stomped away from the farm.

I also help come up with storylines, sometimes by accident. I've always wanted to live on the road—#VanLife—so a few years ago I bought a $500 RV because it was cheap and I thought I could fix everything that was wrong with it. I wanted to get Rich's input on what had to be done, and I knew he would get some good content for his channel, so I invited him up to New Hampshire to take a look at it.

When he saw it, the first thing out of his mouth was "Leenda, what the hell are you doing? This is a meth lab on wheels." He then proceeded to shoot an entire video making fun of my van and pointing out all the things that were wrong with it. But "I Found Out My Assistant Lives in a Dilapidated Van, So This Is What I Did" got almost a million views, which launched the whole van rebuild series.

Making the Sherp videos was lots of fun. We plowed through the woods of his backyard and went through a McDonald's drive-through and were all rolling around in the back because there are no freaking seat belts. There was nothing for me to hold on to, and we just laughed our asses off the whole time.

Once I became a regular character on *Rich Rebuilds*, I studied Rich during every shoot because I knew I could learn a lot from him. After all, I had my own YouTube channel and posted new content there and on Instagram on a regular basis.

Just like *Rich Rebuilds*, my channel is 100 percent authentic. Nothing is staged. I just shoot and figure it out later. With Rich's blessing, I decided to piggyback off his most recent video to make my own version. In other words, whenever Rich posts a new video, I post my own about what went on behind the scenes on my channel the following day. That way, viewers can get two different views of one episode, and they can get to know Rich in a different light.

I've obviously gotten traction off Rich's channel, but our collaboration has created a lot of speculation about his personal life and the nature of our relationship. The questions never end: *Are Leenda and Rich dating? I thought he was married!*

It's funny how people are so quick to assume a man and a woman who regularly appear together in videos are having a relationship. I think it's hilarious because we have such a brother-and-sister dynamic. We're constantly bickering, whether the camera is running or not.

If only people knew what he was really like behind the scenes. To be honest, I don't know how he's able to juggle everything. But I also have to be very mindful of how I address this issue, because I want to protect my brand too. I don't want anyone to think that the reason I'm working with Rich is because I slept my way to the top.

I'm always very honest about how we started working together, but there are still going to be those idiots who don't care and post ludicrous comments. Then again, there are a lot of people who have tuned in only recently, so they haven't watched any early episodes and just assume that we're an item.

Rich here. Leenda has had to deal with some of the same issues that I have, where viewers make up in-depth stories about her life based on nothing. She's had boyfriends all along, but she doesn't talk about her personal life too much. I guess all the men who are her fans want to believe the fantasy that they can be with a girl like that.

So she's learned not to say anything about her relationship status, because that's what pays her bills.

Back to Leenda: My life has totally changed since I first appeared on *Rich Rebuilds*. Yes, it's brought me more exposure and more opportunities, but what I consider to be even more important is what I've learned from working with Rich.

After all, spending time with another creator and watching him work is a great inspiration. You know, if he can do it, I can too. I've been working with him for a few years now, and it's helped to build my résumé and get my foot in several doors.

Being on *Rich Rebuilds* boosted my YouTube audience pretty quickly. I had only about a thousand subscribers when I first appeared on his channel, which jumped to thirty-one thousand within a few months.

I love how Rich teases his audience and drops a few crumbs about his real life, which always sends the Comments section into a frenzy. So I decided this would be a good place to tell you something about him that no one outside of his inner circle knows.

Even though Rich has zillions of followers and produces and stars in a new video on a regular basis, the truth is that IRL he doesn't love being the center of attention. At heart, he's a mix of extrovert and introvert, leaning more heavily toward the latter. In fact, he can be pretty socially awkward, so it's hilarious to see him squirm when the spotlight is on him. He's obviously capable of warming up to people, but there have been a few times at trade shows when fans have approached him and he's been generous, talking with them and signing autographs, but then suddenly a switch will flip and he'll say, "Oh my God, Leenda. Get me out of here."

Rich makes everything look easy, but he works really hard. No one in this business talks about the endless wear and tear of social media and how it can run you down over time. The truth is that being a successful content creator at his level is really difficult, and the cycle of producing and promoting a video is beyond stressful because it never really ends.

Sometimes he hits a creative wall and just needs to reset and pump the brakes. It's the only way to restore some peace and mental clarity. When we first started working together, I had no idea of the pressure he faced every single day. As I saw the toll it took on him, I encouraged him to be more realistic about what he can handle as well as the people he works with, and to be mindful of giving himself the care he needs.

I'm very happy to see him evolving, and I'm very proud to work with Rich.

DRESS FOR SUCCESS

When it comes to my on-camera wardrobe, I wish I could say I put some thought into it, but basically I just grab whatever doesn't smell too bad.

I'm a big sweatshirt guy. One of my favorite sweatshirts is from an Audi repair shop that my friend runs, so I'm advertising his business instead of my own, but I wear it because it's comfortable. I should be wearing my own merch, but it's easier to wear someone else's clothes than to remember to wear my own. I think that's one of the reasons my merch doesn't sell. As a matter of fact, whenever I wear someone else's merch, it makes it unlikely that someone will recognize me in public.

I'm starting to feel like Mark Zuckerberg in a way. He's so busy and his mind is so active that he has no time to think about clothes, so he wears the same thing every day that he picks from a closet full of gray shirts and jeans.

I wish I had the time to sit down and buy more sweatshirts from the '80s and '90s, like the *Full House* one that I often wear on video shoots. If I like a sweatshirt, I'll wear it until it falls apart. I have jeans and sweatshirts from a decade ago, and they're all in bad shape, but I wear them out of nostalgia. I got a lot of these clothes when I was at a different point in my life, and whenever I wear them it reminds me of how far I've come.

In fact, a lot of the things I do today are to prove that I've moved on from an earlier point in my life. When I was working in IT, I bought at least ten pairs of high-end sneakers, the brands that all the cool kids in high school wore. I couldn't afford to buy them when I was a kid, and my father refused to get them for me. Once I was working, I had the money, so I went out and bought all my favorite sneakers.

I bought all those sneakers to relive my childhood, but I wore each pair only once or twice. I still have them, but they're just sitting there. I don't wear them like I thought I would. They're more of a monument to an earlier time in my life, when I wasn't as responsible for stuff as I am now.

THE MAGIC FLUTE

Most viewers have heard the out-of-tune musical note that I use to bleep out curse words in the video.

A lot of people think it's a flute, but it's actually a recorder, a simple woodwind that is a first instrument for many kids, including my oldest daughter, Breanna. When she started playing the recorder, she was so terrible that I couldn't help but laugh. In fact, it was so hilarious that I started dubbing it into the videos.

As she got older, she started getting better at the recorder, and I couldn't use her anymore because it wasn't as funny. I went online and found a guy who plays the recorder poorly on purpose, and I started to dub his audio into the videos.

It's become such a staple in the videos that people come to expect it, though I've expanded its use. When I swear I'll usually just use a quick bleep, but when there's a string of several notes I use it either to convey irony or to foreshadow when something unfortunate is about to happen, as a signal to viewers that it's okay to laugh at me.

One time I used it as background music in a video when I went to the DMV to register a car, and the fees were so insane I almost choked. It was one of those first world problems: I'm literally registering a $100,000 car, so why should anyone feel bad for me?

I also use the bad recorder to poke fun at myself because I live a lifestyle that most people don't, so if something bad happens to me, it's not that bad. My life is not terrible, so I can only laugh at myself, and I want you guys to laugh at me too.

CHAPTER FOURTEEN

HORSE SEX

As things turned out, I didn't have to worry about becoming irrelevant, because one day in the summer of 2022, the phone rang, and Joe Rogan invited me to come on his show.

Again.

Apparently, he doesn't invite many guests back a second time. The first time I went on the show was because he wanted to talk about Dolores. It was right up his alley because he loves guests who are into science, engineering, and technology. This time he wanted to talk about ICE-T.

In the three years since I had first appeared on the show, my entire life had changed. When Rogan called this time, I had well over a million subscribers. In fact, to celebrate that milestone, I had taken the wife of my millionth subscriber— actually, it was my 1,000,004th subscriber, since some didn't want to play along—out to Olive Garden. I was shocked at the numbers that video drew: twice as many viewers as my usual build videos.

I also hit number one on my bucket list: appearing in a six-page, full-color feature in the September 2020 issue of *Car and Driver* magazine. More than any of my other media appearances or videos, the article gave me instant respectability in a field where it is often in short supply.

Of course, I wanted to go on Rogan's show again, but when the producer asked if I could appear on a specific day, I had to tell him no. I was crazy busy, juggling several builds along with a few other projects, and I couldn't just drop everything to fly out to do the show.

I knew I was taking a big risk. They might say, "No, sorry, it's this day or forget it." But with three years of success and independence under my belt, I felt empowered. After all, this was how I provided for my family, by producing content. In a way, I felt like Rogan and I were on a similar level now. We both put on a show and entertain people, only he does it on a much larger scale and is a lot more successful than I am.

The first time I went on the show, I looked up to him and was extremely intimidated by him. Now I viewed us more as equals, playing the same game on different levels.

So I said, "How about a month from now?"

No problem, and we booked the date.

I flew to the studio in Austin and settled in. When the ON AIR light came on, a rush of nerves hit me just like the first time, but I quickly calmed down since I knew what to expect. We talked about cars for about twenty minutes or so, and then somehow we veered off into unexpected territory and started to talk about bestiality and having sex with horses.

I knew it was a test. Joe and his producers were just waiting for me to curl up into a ball and start sputtering and say, "I'm uncomfortable with this. I've had enough."

But I've always been willing to talk with anyone about literally any topic, so I just followed his lead. It was a little weird, but it was also pretty funny, so I hung in there.

Afterward, everyone called to tell me they couldn't believe what we'd talked about and how disgusting it was, but I had learned that if you want to get to a higher level, you have to know how to roll with the punches, and that's exactly what I did.

I don't care who you are; we're all afraid of something. Most of us are afraid of the unknown or how something will make us look and what other people will think. But I think that many people are afraid simply because they haven't thought through the steps required to do something. Once they accomplish something they haven't done before, they'll feel more competent, which will encourage them to try bigger things.

Baby steps.

In fact, I think it's easy to take control of your life by fixing something on a very small scale. Once you succeed at a small task, the feeling of accomplishment is the best trophy you'll ever get.

Here's an example. When I met my wife Allison, she constantly worried about anything that could go wrong: What if *this* happens? What if *that* happens? One day we were driving somewhere and the empty fuel tank light came on, and her anxiety went through the roof. "How can you keep driving?" she asked, her voice at a fever pitch. "What if we run out of gas?"

I told her that we weren't going to run out of gas, because I know my car. I've calculated it, and once that light turns on, I know exactly how much longer I can go depending on how I'm driving. If I'm driving efficiently, I have between seven and ten miles left. If I'm driving like a jerk, I have three. Six if I'm driving in the middle.

While she was freaking out, I asked her some basic worst-case-scenario questions to try and calm her down: *What if we do run out of gas? What do you think will happen?*

"Then we can't get where we're going."

"Well, where *are* we going?" There wasn't any place that we really needed to be that day, and we weren't on a schedule. It was broad daylight and we weren't in a bad neighborhood, so we were okay.

"And if we *do* run out of gas?"

"We'll call AAA and they'll bring us gas," I said. Or we could use our phone to find the nearest gas station and walk over to buy a gas can and a gallon of gas, or we could call a Lyft to bring it to us. Then we'd be on our way.

Today, she's almost as laid-back as I am . . . almost. After all, she drove Dolores for several years, and let me tell you that range anxiety is leagues beyond the fear of running out of gas. In fact, she's only called me once when she was low on charge, with about five miles left, and the nearest charging station ten miles away.

I told her to turn off the heat, shut the headlights, and go easy on the accelerator. If she didn't make it to the station, then we'd figure out what to do next.

People never think about the real risks. Instead, they're so afraid of what could go wrong that they never even try anything new. It can be as simple as learning to patch a hole in the wall or pulling an engine from a '74 GTO. It can be deciding to change your life in either a very small or an earth-shattering way. Either way, the following principles—and questions—can be applied to anything you're considering.

First, assess the risk. What is the greatest risk? And what's your biggest fear about what will happen if you screw up? In other words, what does failure look like to you? If you fail, will your life be over? Probably not. Okay then, are you scared that failure will reveal even more things that need to be fixed, or that everyone will make fun of you? Are you scared that you'll do such a bad job, that it will cost you money...or your pride?

Then, keep going. What kind of satisfaction would you get out of doing it yourself? How do you think you'll feel after it's done, whether you've fixed it or not? In a way, all the questions I'm posing here are akin to therapy. After all, everything in life involves risk, even choosing not to take a risk. And what's the worst that could happen afterward, when you discover whether you were comfortable taking a risk... or not?

After all, life is just a matter of weighing your options, because as careless as I appear, everything I do is a calculated risk. To me, risk is always worth it, because so many of the things we do on a day-to-day basis don't present us with tangible results. With this method, even if you don't succeed at the task, at least you've answered your question, which is always a measurable accomplishment in my book.

I've lived my entire life this way. Well, most of the time. I admit that sometimes I'm pretty lousy at taking my own advice. I'd be lying if I said I didn't worry about the future of *Rich Rebuilds*. Some weeks I'm juggling so much between builds, insurance, sponsors, and video editing that I'm so stressed that even *I* don't want to be around me. Some nights it takes me hours to turn off my brain enough so I can fall asleep while all my worries are coursing through my head. Whenever I get too bent out of shape, I apply the same process and try to answer the questions I've been torturing myself with. The one that is never too far from my consciousness is: *What will happen if YouTube stops tomorrow?*

Well, maybe I'll get a break for a change.

What if you make less money?

I know how much I have to bring in every month to keep the ship sailing, but if I don't, I think about what my family and I really need to survive. In a way, my cars are my savings account, so I could sell some cars and go from there.

But you'll have to change your lifestyle!

Yes, but no one ever asks the question "Do you really need this lifestyle, or can you live with less?" Many people are scared of moving down the ladder, because they equate their sense of well-being with money and status and believe it reflects poorly on them if they fail. Again, I know I'm an outlier since I am always able to see value in failure—and even welcome it in many cases—but I think if people could learn to focus on what's really important in life that they could adjust to living below their means if they had to.

What about saving for retirement?

Whenever I tell someone I don't have a 401(k), they think there's something seriously wrong with me. "But you have to have a 401(k)! And a college fund for the kids!" I know all this, of course, but there's no arguing with them. Instead I tell them, "You know what? You're right. But I have a video due tomorrow."

My oldest is halfway through her physician assistant program at a prestigious pharmacy school in the heart of Boston, which I pay for, and she drives a special car—Dolores—every day to school, so I suppose that I kind of figured it out.

I've seen many people who don't have to worry about money spend way too much time working instead of spending time with their family. "Sorry, kid, I didn't get to see you very much because I was busy working, but look at all the money that I have to show for it." That's really awesome, but when you die with $1 million in the bank, that means someone else is going to drive a fancy sports car on your dime. You should have been enjoying that money and that time with your kids and your family, but now that you're on your way out, someone else is going to. Was it really worth it? What was all that hard work really for?

If there's one thing I hate, it's being told what to do. I didn't work this hard and come this far just for some guy to tell me what time I have to be somewhere or how much they're going to pay me.

And that includes sponsors and companies that send me a product that they want me to mention in a video.

Yes, sponsors help pay the bills, and the overwhelming majority are more than happy to leave it up to me to come up with the best way to mention their product in a video. But when somebody tells me that they have a product that is going to make my channel explode and that they'll pay me a lot of money if I review it in the next video, I usually walk away. Sometimes it's because I don't like the product, but more often it's because I don't like the person's attitude. Plus, I don't like being rushed. When I turn the sponsor down, nine times out of ten, out comes the money carrot: "But we'll pay you twice as much."

Personally, I love it when someone dangles the money carrot because I love telling them that I don't care about their money...and then seeing their reaction. Once they lose their sole leverage point, they realize they have no power. There are so many people who think they can use money to manipulate others. I've never been one of them, so it's been a real eye-opener.

I've already mentioned that my business partner Chad thinks I'm a cat, and that I've used up some of my nine lives working on Dolores and the other cars.

I like to take the metaphor one step further: If I'm a cat and I fall three stories, I'll still land on my feet. I'll be a little bumped and bruised, but I'll be okay. The bonus is that I now know how to fall off a building, because if that building's on fire, some of the other cats probably aren't going to make it. But since I already know how to jump, there's a good chance that I will survive.

I don't think ten years ahead. I don't even think five years ahead. All I think is *I'll figure it out and it's going to be okay.* Worst-case scenario: I could make the coffee and sweep floors at the Electrified Garage. It would actually be a lot less stressful, because as fun as making a video is, sometimes I don't want to. Sometimes I want to take a week, or a whole month, off, but I can't because there are people who depend on me. If I'm not making money, I can't pay them, and then it would turn into a very scary cycle.

In a way, I've created my own rat race. In the normal rat race, you get up, take the train, fight traffic, and work for someone else. Then you come home and do it all again the next day. The difference now is that I'm only competing with myself. After all, there's no one telling me to do this or that, but I *am* on a treadmill, and I do need to drop a new video every so often.

Running *Rich Rebuilds* is a job—and it's the best job ever—but sometimes I feel overwhelmed and need to remind myself to keep things in perspective. On those days, if there's a foot of snow outside, I think, *Well, at least I don't have to get in my car and drive into Boston.* Or I think about the fact that I can spend time with my kids in the morning and drive them to school. I also don't have a boss breathing down my neck. At the same time, I should probably get up and start working because if I don't work, I *will* have a boss breathing down my neck, so my desire to stay out of the rat race is part of my motivation for getting up each day.

SUPERFANS

I define a *superfan* as a person who goes way beyond the scope of a regular fan. Their skills include the ability to memorize dates, episodes, and other trivia that rivals my own knowledge.

And yes, I have them.

When I first got Dolores, I had to charge her using a wall outlet in my garage because I didn't have the money to have an electrician install a Tesla wall charger. A full charge took about three days.

I never thought that a complete stranger could be so invested in me and the channel, but one day a man named George from New York—aka Jojo—emailed me to tell me that I had inspired him to purchase and rebuild a Tesla model S, just like Dolores.

George loved his car and said he wanted to thank me by giving me a brand-new Tesla wall charger. Plus, he'd help install it.

At first, I thought it was a scam, but I decided to take a chance.

He showed up and helped me drill through three inches of concrete to install the charger, which is described in my video "Unprofessionals Guide to Installing a Tesla Wall Connector," posted on June 1, 2018. After that, it took only a few hours to charge Dolores, and George and I have become good friends. We talk regularly, and he still sends me gifts that I'll use in videos as gags.

ON LETTING GO

It's almost impossible for me to sell a car.

In fact, I rarely sell them. If I get attached to a car, I give it a name and then I really can't sell it. It's why most farmers don't name their animals. And now that I'm a public figure, at least in the automotive world, it's even harder for me to sell for a couple of reasons. First, I've built my cars to be very catchy and grab the eye. Second, most of the cars have been featured on at least a few videos, so the likelihood of selling one without someone knowing who owned it is pretty low. And third, since I'm known as a car rebuilder, if a car doesn't meet a new owner's standards of a car that's been rebuilt, then they will happily make that information public.

The other reason I cannot let my babies out into the wild is because whoever gets their hands on a car that I've sweated over is going to want to critique it on their own YouTube channel. I don't want to be immodest, but it would definitely boost their ratings, and they'd certainly pay a premium for the car. And then they'd proceed to tear it apart: "Hey, guess what? I have a car that Rich Rebuilds worked on, so let me show you all the duct tape he used everywhere." I'd forever be associated with that car.

Right now, I'm embarrassed to admit that I don't know how many cars I actually have. They take up room and it's kind of annoying, but I have them stored at my friends' houses, my dad's house, and my mom's house. They're scattered all over the United States pretty much. Happily, right now I don't really have to sell any of the cars. But mostly I hold on to a car because I like it.

CHAPTER FIFTEEN

GAME OVER

I use the phrase GAME OVER a lot. I even have it on a license plate: GMEOVR.

For me, it has multiple meanings.

First—and I know this is going to sound bad—I don't let my family get in my way. I just don't.

Stay with me here.

As I've described, before I was born, my mother always wanted a Corvette. She saved up a whole bunch of money to buy one, but before she could get it, she got very sick. She went to the hospital, and a doctor said that she was sick because she was pregnant.

With me.

As a result, she never got that Corvette. So when I was able to buy my own Corvette, I considered it to be my tribute to her.

I still have it today, and even though I have much better driving and riding cars, I have a soft spot in my heart for that car. Every time I drive it, I think of my mother and how much she gave up for me.

But I almost didn't buy it because, at the time, I couldn't afford it. Allison and I weren't married, and we owned our first multifamily building together. Our son had just turned one.

Then I thought, *Why not?* My mother always regretted not buying the Corvette, and I never want to regret anything. So I told Allison I wanted to buy a Camaro, and she was on board from the beginning. It was a great car, with four seats, big enough for a family to cruise around in. I looked around for a Camaro, found one in Florida, and flew down. When I got there, I saw the coolest Corvette Z06 in the lot and instantly decided that I no longer wanted a Camaro. I wanted that Corvette, because it was sportier and also because I knew my mother would love driving it.

It only had two seats, but it didn't matter. I bought the Corvette and headed north.

I was about five minutes away from home when I called Allison and told her to bring our son out front. I pulled up in the Corvette, and she peered inside. "Where's the back seat?"

"What back seat?"

"You said the car had a back seat."

"Oh, that was the Camaro. I decided to get the Corvette instead."

Did I mention that she was pregnant with our second child at the time?

She just rolled her eyes.

When my friends heard about it, they thought I was effing crazy. "You're going to be a father of three, and you just bought this car that none of your kids can ride in?"

I admit this sounds extremely selfish, but I've never really let my family get in the way, because I know what's going to happen. A big reason why I needed that Corvette so badly was because, with two kids and another on the way, it felt like the window on the cool side of my life was closing, and a sports car would help prop it open for just a little longer.

I know it sounds bad, but GAME OVER is also a little nudge to those who just gave up. Take any guy who drives a Honda Odyssey minivan with one of those stick-family stickers on the rear window showing how many kids he has. You have twelve kids? Trust me, no one cares, and that sticker is basically telling the world that the game—and therefore your life—is over. You disagree? Well, no one told you to have that many.

I've heard far too many stories about guys who had a cool car, but when they had kids they had to sell the car to buy a minivan. It didn't take long for them to start resenting their family. I've never wanted to be that person. After all, I was here first, before my kids, and I'll continue to live the life that I've always lived.

Fortunately, my kids think it's cool, and thankfully my wife is used to me by now. I know I'm very fortunate because many women wouldn't be happy with a husband like me. My family allows me to follow my dreams, but at the same time, it's not a one-way thing; they also have the freedom to pursue their own dreams. The kids don't get in the way because they love what I do.

I'm a very lucky man.

Another definition of GAME OVER is that it's time to get to work. After all, as cool as the cars are, they have to be paid for.

But even more, GAME OVER means that nothing lasts forever.

As I've said, I'm at the upper limit, age-wise, of a successful automotive YouTuber. While I could easily crank nonstop for twelve hours a day when I started the channel, that's no longer the case.

Nor do I want to, so I've been slowly pulling back in terms of how much time I spend working. Don't get me wrong, I still spend most of my waking hours working on the channel and thinking up possible builds for future videos. But I have to take mental breaks to recharge, and I've even started to go up to three weeks without posting a new video. Some of my fans don't like it, but it's the only way I can continue.

Another problem that many automotive YouTubers face is that, because we love cars, sometimes there's a thin line between love and obligation. If I didn't have a YouTube channel, I'd still spend hours working on cars. But now before I pick the next car for a build, I have to make sure it's something that other people will like too. For example, many YouTubers will pick a particular car to feature just because it's trending, and I will admit that I've sometimes been guilty of this in the past to keep feeding the machine. But I've always ended up resenting it, so it's definitely GAME OVER for that.

Which is why you probably won't see a Mazda Miata on the channel.

Occupational hazard: it's hard to enjoy the cars I do have, because there's always another car on the horizon. I love my Sherp and the 911, but I never drive them because I'm so busy working on the next video. And viewers have made it clear that they don't really care about the Sherp anymore, so I can't justify making another video on it. Besides, it would probably bore me.

When I take a break or go on vacation, it's hard to get out of influencer mode. Sadly, if I can't film content, then it's almost not worth doing. Once we took the kids to a water park in New York, and even though I know how to swim, I'd rather avoid the water. So instead, I spent the afternoon in the parking lot, shooting a charging session with the Rivian.

I sometimes beat myself up for this, but in a way it all goes back to childhood. I'll forever be taking things apart so I can learn what makes them tick. After all, I'm still the same person I was when I first sat behind the wheel of a Model S, or when I took apart my mom's VCR for that matter. But it's funny how the world works. You don't really know what your path is until you start. If you're truly meant to do something, if it is your destiny, then it will happen.

For example, I could have defied my father and insisted on becoming a mechanic instead of going to college. If I didn't get a degree in computer science, maybe I wouldn't have been so taken with Teslas.

When I started my YouTube channel, there were maybe about ten thousand Teslas on the road. Today, there are three million, so if you just bought your first Tesla, there are hundreds of channels and websites to tell you everything you need to know, which is great for Tesla drivers but not for content creators.

In a way, I'm back to the crabs in a bucket analogy my father warned me about, because on YouTube—and Instagram and TikTok and Facebook—everyone is trying to step on someone else to get to the next level.

You hear so many stories about celebrities treating other people like garbage. I heard a story about someone who presented a late-night talk show host with a question, and if he couldn't answer it, then he would have to eat some really terrible food.

The question: Can you tell me the first name of one of your camerapeople?

Of course he couldn't answer it, so he ended up eating the disgusting food, which was fish urine or something crazy like that.

That is *not* Robert Downey Jr. When we were first introduced on the set of *Downey's Dream Cars*, he said hi to me and asked how my family and kids were doing. He was friendly to everyone. He's literally an A-lister, but he's not a jerk or a diva. He doesn't say, "Hey, where's my water? Where's my latte?" I've seen YouTubers act more diva-like than he does.

At the same time, he was definitely the commanding presence in the room. I don't know if that's the role he's playing or if that's just who he is naturally, but what also struck me was how calm and down-to-earth he was.

We started shooting *Downey's Dream Cars* in August 2021, almost two years before it first aired, and most of the time we were on set we were constantly surrounded by people: producers, videographers, assistants, other guys working on the cars.

Very little of the show was scripted, which surprised the hell out of me, and we didn't rehearse anything in advance. The producers told us where to stand but not what to say, which I appreciated because it allowed us to be more natural. Sometimes, I got a little too detailed with my descriptions when I was explaining something, and the producer told me to dumb it down a bit. But a lot of my weird, slightly perverse humor came out, and thankfully they left most of it in—like when I cracked a joke about playing with Chad's tools—so that was pretty refreshing to see.

Of course, the entire process was the opposite of how I make my videos, where I literally walk into the shop, say hi to the guys, turn the camera on, and start the conversation. Then again, I'm not spending thousands of dollars per hour on a production crew, and in my case, we tend not to do multiple takes. I've never said to do a retake because you didn't say this right or you farted while you were talking. From my perspective, I think, *Oh, you farted? Even better.*

And if there's a second season, I'm there.

A couple of months ago, my son's soccer team lost their championship match, but everyone on the team still got a trophy.

I had a hard time with that because, no offense, kid, but you lost. The team you went up against was the superior team, so you shouldn't get a trophy.

Right now, we live in a culture where everyone gets a trophy, which I think is a by-product of our disposable society. If there's a hole in the wall you need to patch, and you can't do it—or don't want to learn how to do it—who's going to give you a trophy? As a result, if something doesn't work, most people just throw it out and buy another one.

The problem is that you're the only one who can give yourself that trophy and pat yourself on the back. A lot of the time, people start pointing fingers at others and say, "Well, you didn't give me the right hammer," or "You didn't do this." They're always looking for someone else to blame. But if it's only you, that's a lot harder. And people are scared to do things by themselves.

Then again, it's not entirely their fault.

On social media, most people like to paint a rosy picture that everything's perfect: look how white my teeth are/how big my muscles are/how smart my kids are. Of course, the viewers don't see any context or how lives have been manipulated and airbrushed to present that perfect picture.

They don't see that this guy has a $75,000 credit card balance or $200,000 in student loans or that woman hasn't spoken with her parents in years.

I think that a lot of people see these perfect people online and decide to model their lives on them. Of course, this is destined to fail, and because everyone online looks so happy, you start to think you're a failure when your life doesn't magically change. So you post a photo where you *look* like you're happy, and if you get a lot of likes maybe then you won't feel so dead on the inside.

Rinse and repeat.

We live in a society where everyone gets a trophy for losing and thousands of likes for posting a totally fake picture, so it's no wonder that people are terrified of failure. After all, admitting to failure online is tantamount to suicide, though as I've said, my videos tend to attract more viewers when I screw up. But when the focus of someone's channel is themselves and they fail in some way, viewers tend to desert the sinking ship because it forces them to look at their own life—and maybe even though other people think it's perfect, they know it's as flimsy as a house of cards in a windstorm.

I'm not saying that I've been immune to the magical thinking that comes from being an online success. But because I've actually believed some of these things and have seen firsthand that making money and being relatively famous in some circles doesn't instantly improve your life, I feel particularly justified to speak out against it.

I also think that social media has exposed a lot of things about myself that I wasn't ready for. I now know that I have an ego and that I'm self-conscious about things. I think that social media, specifically the Comments section, has brought a lot of those things out.

In the beginning, I'd read every single comment. With a potentially controversial video, the comments are bittersweet because they can either engage me and make me want to do more, or they can tear me down to the point where I never want to log into YouTube again. Today, I rarely read the comments because they can bring me down very fast.

Even though I have a team of professionals and friends working with me, most of the time I feel lonely. I spend the bulk of my waking hours by myself, and, ironically, social media has made me feel more alone than ever.

What's the solution to feeling lonely on social media? I don't know. After all, one of the reasons you go online is to not feel lonely. It's very strange how social media rewires your brain. And as much as I want to get away and take a break, I don't know what to do if I don't have my phone, because then I have to be with my own thoughts, and that's a scary place to be.

Of course, I shouldn't complain about these things because I'm pretty successful. Everyone sees the toys and the cars and thinks my life is perfect. In reality, it's far from it. I frequently ask myself, *Am I doing the right thing? Is this the life I want to live?*

Maybe everyone asks these questions at one point or another.

Or maybe the root cause is that no one knows how to do anything that doesn't involve making a video or snapping a photo anymore, myself included. And if you screw up on camera, just hit the Delete button.

I don't know what the answer is. For me, if something doesn't work, I'm still okay because I've learned something new.

I'll tell you what matters most to me these days. Back in the summer of 2021, Miss Mariota Theodoris, the STEM coordinator of the Urban League of Palm Beach, got in touch to let me know that the African American elementary school kids she worked with had watched some of my videos as part of their lessons, and she wanted to know if I could take a few minutes to answer six questions from the students about my background.

I was a bit taken aback at the thought of kids watching my videos, but I wanted to see these kids for myself. After all, when I was their age, I would have loved to talk with an adult who looked like me who could answer my questions about science.

I invited them to take a tour of the Electrified Garage that had just opened in West Palm Beach and told Miss Mariota—as the kids referred to her—that I wanted to do a Zoom call so I could talk to them face-to-face.

From the moment I logged on, I was a total mess. It's not common for me to be surrounded by people who look like me, especially in my field. The kids told me what they wanted to be when they grew up and asked how they could follow their dreams just like I did. One little girl told me that she wanted to study astronomy because she loves learning about stars, and she asked me how she could approach her parents because her father told her she couldn't make any money that way.

After I answered their questions, I told the kids that they should all be very, very proud of themselves for wanting to pursue a STEM career—or really for pursuing anything. After all, it's all about the pursuit! And then I said I wanted them all to be so smart and successful that I would work for one of them someday.

After I logged off, I didn't think I'd spontaneously bawl my eyes out in a Taco Bell drive-through, but there I was. When I watched the video later, they all reminded me of myself when I was a young bear cub.

It was one of the most gratifying and emotional events of my entire life. And I'd love to do more of these talks with young people who are just as curious as I was when I was that age, whether they look like me or not.

I've always been weird because, if I can dream it or think it, I know I can achieve it. It's always been my superpower, and I totally acknowledge that very few people have been raised with this outlook. I've been very fortunate.

I don't often think about how far I've come. After all, it was only a few years ago that I was working at a desk job, and now I have millions of people who are interested in me and what I'm doing.

Asking the question *What's next?* has long been my default. It's served me very well in creating a successful YouTube channel. After all, I always have to think about the next video, the next project, the next sponsor. I get an Audi, work on the Audi, finish the Audi, then the Audi is gone. I buy a flooded Tesla, fix it, and it's onto the next project. Rinse and repeat.

It can sometimes get a bit tedious, so I try to shake things up. In 2021, I decided to increase the number of sponsors for each video. When I started *Rich Rebuilds*, the rule of thumb was one sponsor per video. In the beginning, I didn't question it, but as I became more popular and new companies asked to advertise, I had to turn them down because I was already booked up months in advance.

Then it hit me: *Who made this rule? Why can't I have two sponsors in the video?* I could make more capital to fund the projects, as they were getting astronomically more expensive. So I told potential sponsors that they could serve as a secondary sponsor, appearing later in the video and paying a lower rate, since only 30 percent of viewers will watch a video until the end. This worked for everyone: the primary sponsor got the first slot, the second sponsor appeared sooner rather than later, and I could afford the builds.

In recent years, the *What's next?* question has started to become a problem. I've asked myself more questions: *Is there more to life than an endless cycle of a shiny new build that looks tarnished when it's done? Does everybody go through this when they turn forty?*

If I'm honest with myself, I don't think I'll ever stop asking these questions. They're both part of my identity.

What I do know is that I'll never stop pushing the envelope to see what I can get away with. I've had to leave a lot out of this book so that the local constables don't come down on me, so for now I've restricted my resistance to asking if I can say something in a video without getting canceled or if I can do a certain build without getting in trouble or breaking the law.

Most of the time.

I've always believed that, as crazy as this world is and as bad as things can get, the best way to fight the bad with the good is by being kind to people. If you can make someone's day, you've already changed the world for the better, whether it's teaching someone something, complimenting someone on their abs, or taking time out of your day to call an old friend. And while it may not be everyone's cup of tea, to me that includes raising happy, successful, productive children.

What can I leave behind? Money? No, I bought that Porsche, remember? After all, I won't be here forever, so I always think, *What can I give back?* Long after I'm gone, and long after people stop watching my videos and my cars are rusting into the ground, at least my kids will be part of my legacy.

In the meantime, maybe you've told yourself you want to wait a year or two before buying your dream car. Or maybe you want a new car with the latest technology.

Here's a news flash: all new cars are already out-of-date the first time you sit in them. In fact, technology is moving so fast that your brand-new car will be obsolete before it even rolls off the assembly line.

The best time to buy the car you want is now.

The best time to do something you want to do is now.

What are you waiting for? Life is short and I'm constantly reminded of that every day, of just how short and precious this life is.

You could die tomorrow.

Buy the damn car.

HOW TO SUCCEED ON YOUTUBE

I frequently get asked for advice on how to create and build a successful YouTube channel, both from prospective YouTubers and from those who have several times more subscribers than me.

You wouldn't believe the level of anxiety out there. No matter what their level, they're all worried about the future. So here's my two cents.

Don't create a YouTube channel because you want to be famous, because right now becoming a YouTube star is like Hollywood: for every person who makes it, there are fifty thousand others who fail.

Don't do it for the money. Do it because you personally enjoy it. Do it because you want to show the world what you're capable of doing, because if you go into it solely to chase the money, you're going to be very disappointed. Because there are so many more channels launching every day, viewership has dropped across the board.

Don't do it because you want to be Mr. Popular, because even though there will be more people in your life if your channel hits it big, odds are that they're attracted to you because of what you've been able to accomplish and not because of who you are. Believe me, that gets very old very quickly.

There are many channels that are far better than mine, with better editing, better storylines, and better characters. The people who run them are ten times smarter than me, and no one knows who they are. In fact, the best how-tos and instructional videos that I've seen come from a guy who has a really crappy phone and can barely speak English, but he takes viewers through a series of clearly explained steps on how he fixed his car. It's very low-tech, but it gives me exactly what I'm looking for. He's doing it because he clearly loves it, and nothing is forced.

Maybe I've just turned into the old man yelling at the kids to get off his lawn, but I was thrilled when I got my first subscriber because I wanted to show everyone what I was capable of doing and tell them that they could do this too.

In contrast, too many channels today are just flash and dash. *Hey, look at me and my car. Aren't we cool? Now look at the tool I'm using. Thanks, Company X, for this tool.*

Do it because it's a personal passion of yours, and it'll be longer and more consistent. Success is not how many subscribers you have or how much money you're making. Rather, it's how what you're doing is making you grow.

MASH IT UP

If you've made it this far, congratulations. I'm gonna let you in on a little secret.

My outer shell is made of brick. The second layer is aluminum, and the next is titanium.

It's all covering up nothing but mashed potatoes. Yes, I am absolute mush underneath everything. The hardest, most secure surface is covering the softest, so there ain't nothing that's getting in. At least that's what I tell myself.

I've always thought that all comedians have some level of trauma in them, which they express through jokes. I think a lot of the things they say aren't really jokes, but how they feel inside disguised as a joke.

I'm not sure what I'm protecting. Maybe I don't want to know. Or maybe I just don't want anyone to know that underneath I'm a big softie. I think I'm trying to protect the little kid inside me who doesn't want to be exposed. I consider myself to be a comedian, a sad clown of sorts, trying to make others feel happy because I can't always make myself happy.

My kids are always telling me that they know nothing about me. I talk to my friends and it's the same thing: "I know nothing about you," they say. As social and outgoing as I am, people don't really know me personally, and I didn't understand until now that I don't really give it up. I give up selective information, and I usually do it as a twisted joke, like a mean or funny thing.

Of course, over time you have to do some tuck-pointing on the bricks, because eventually it's going to crack. No structure lasts forever. But as far as I'm concerned, nobody's ever going to see the mashed potatoes.

APPENDIX

DIY BEST PRACTICE
SAFETY FIRST

You only have to watch a few of my early videos to realize that I haven't always taken the proper precautions when working on a car.

Because I always wear regular glasses, I never felt like I had to wear safety glasses or cover my face whenever I used a grinder. As a result, the metal shards would fly everywhere, including behind my glasses and into my eyes. Once that happened, I couldn't work for the rest of the day and had to lie down, put a few eye drops in, and hold a magnet up to my eye until it pulled the metal out.

Yes, it's as disgusting as it sounds.

One time, I couldn't get all the metal out. It took a couple of days of moving my eyes around so the tiny shards could resurface enough to pull them out. I couldn't work until this happened because the more I opened and closed my eyes, the more the metal scratched my eye. It finally hit me that I could work a lot better if I just wore safety goggles when I'm cutting and grinding things.

In 2023, I started working with different people who actually put safety first. My friend Joey is a safety coordinator at his workplace, and he liked to tell me about accidents that happened because someone wasn't wearing the right piece of equipment and suffered some pretty serious damage.

I started to feel a little ashamed that he took precautions and I didn't. For years, I thought I was invincible, that nothing was going to happen to me. Remember, I was the guy who pulled a waterlogged battery pack from a Tesla with his bare hands, among countless other risks.

But as I watched Joey put on safety goggles and hearing protection, it hit me that one day my luck was probably going to run out. Plus, I'm getting older. I built that Tesla years ago when I was a younger man. Today, when I get out of bed, my knees crack and my back hurts in addition to a lot of other stuff. So I thought that maybe it was time I took my health and longevity a little bit more seriously.

I put on the goggles and inserted the earplugs and immediately thought, *Holy crap!* I'm grinding something and my ears aren't bleeding anymore. I can actually sleep at night now because my ears aren't ringing, and I can move my eyes without permanently embedding metal shards in them.

Which is actually kind of cool.

DIY BEST PRACTICE
EXPECTATION MANAGEMENT

Life happens. Life throws curveballs at you.

No matter what you're working on—fixing up a car, finding a new job, or writing a book—I think it's a good rule of thumb to expect everything to take twice as long and cost three times as much. Also, don't think you're going to win every time, because chances are good that you'll lose several times before you win.

I refer to it as expectation management. That way, you won't be disappointed.

Here's one example: I bought an Audi e-tron, an electric vehicle, which had been underwater just like Dolores. I decided to make a video where I'd build a plywood box big enough to hold the car and then fill it with rice, just like what you do with a waterlogged cell phone. It would make a great video and everyone would immediately get it.

Besides, I know everything. I'm the man. The price of the car was way up there, an insane amount of money to spend on an experiment. But you know what? The car spent a few days buried in rice, and after I did a few more things to it, I was able to get the car working, which was awesome. It took just about the amount of time that I thought it would.

I planned to sell it because that's how I recoup some of the money I spend to make a video, but then my unrealistic expectations managed to get in the way. I tried to sell it on Facebook Marketplace, but after a couple of conversations went back and forth, the potential buyer ghosted. *Oh, this is the car that was in rice. I don't want to buy this car. There are probably rice grains everywhere.* So I've officially shot myself in the foot because now that car is infamous, and no one—I repeat, no one—will ever want to purchase it.

Like I said, expectation management.

DIY BEST PRACTICE
ONE TOOL

If you could only have one tool in your desert-island arsenal, I would say it should be a vise grip because, when it comes to working on cars, it's like a Swiss Army knife. You could use it as a hammer or a wrench, and because it has sharp teeth, you could use it to cut something. You could also use it to hold things steady or take things apart.

It's a pretty versatile tool and can do stuff that you haven't even thought of yet. One day, I was driving an old BMW 5 Series that I had bought for $500 and was planning to flip. All of a sudden it shut down, and I discovered that the negative ground on the battery was loose. I needed to tighten it enough that I could drive home, and I just happened to have a vise grip with me. I secured the ground to the battery with the vise grip, the car started right up, and off I went.

In fact, it worked so well that I forgot about it and soon sold the car. Six months later, the new owner texted to tell me that he'd found the vise grip when he went to change the battery, and we both had a good laugh.

DIY BEST PRACTICE
FIXING YOUR CAR

Hands down, the one thing in a car that will alarm most people who aren't mechanically inclined is when the CHECK ENGINE light comes on. The flip side is that most people who *are* comfortable working on cars will just ignore it, sometimes for days, even weeks, until they get around to dealing with it.

Here's a general rule of thumb: If the CHECK ENGINE light comes on and your car starts and runs and drives, it's just letting you know that the car isn't feeling so good but that you're probably okay. But if the light is flashing, you're on borrowed time and you need to get to a garage pronto, because there's a good chance that your car might not start the next time you turn it on.

Mechanics generally get a bad rap, and of course there are those who prey on car owners who don't know what a dipstick is for, but there's a really easy way to arm yourself with some knowledge. You can do it with a code reader, a diagnostic tool that you can plug into your car that will tell you exactly what the problem is. Even better, you don't need to buy your own. Most auto parts stores will plug one into your car for free. Then you can tell the mechanic what the code reader said, which may make it less likely that you'll be taken advantage of.

As with everything in life, a little knowledge often goes a long way.

DIY BEST PRACTICE
DEALING WITH PEOPLE

When I was younger, I loved to be around people. I wanted to talk to everyone and be their new best friend. But ever since I started doing YouTube, that's kind of gone away because I've discovered that a lot of people are just basically terrible: they're envious, they're jealous, they're racist, they're whatever. And I just don't want to talk to them.

I've also learned that sometimes friendships just kind of fade into the abyss. It can turn out that we're not on the same path anymore, so it's okay to go our separate ways. I've actually done that. This may sound bad, but I have friends I no longer talk to because they remind me of who I used to be. Since I'm always trying to grow, I don't really want to associate with them anymore because it feels like they'll drag me back to being the person I was before.

Harsh, I know, but I've also discovered that you don't have to like everyone and not everyone has to like you. I think, a lot of the time, we work so hard to get people to accept us and it's so unnecessary because you could be the juiciest, ripest peach in the whole world and you'll still find someone who hates peaches. I think that's the best piece of advice I can give.

DIY BEST PRACTICE
TAKING TIME FOR YOURSELF

I think no matter what stage of life you're in, there will always be someone who wants something from you.

Whether it's because your boss needs a report from you, or your college professor wants a paper, or your spouse or partner asks you to check off something on the honey-do list, it's impossible to go through life without having someone ask you to do something for them.

Most of the time people are willing to help, but many don't grasp the fact that each and every time that someone asks you to do something, a very small piece of you breaks off because, after all, it's your time that you're giving up. We all have a finite amount of time to spend on this earth, and when someone asks you to give up your own time to serve them, that's time that you'll never, ever get back.

Of course, I've learned this the hard way. And the truth is that a lot of the demands that people make of you really aren't that important. Taking time for myself is extremely important. Sitting down in a quiet room and being able to reflect is huge. I think it's important to block off hours or even an entire day when you don't answer your phone or check email.

Every day I set aside some time to get quiet so I can ask myself a few questions: *How am I feeling today? What's bothering me? What good things are happening in my life right now?* I've been doing this for a while, and I can't explain what it does, but it helps me feel more at ease because I'm verbalizing what my fears are, why I'm happier, or why things aren't really going my way. And as the day goes on, I somehow process these answers, and I can often figure out why something is happening and then move on from it.

ACKNOWLEDGMENTS

Dan Ambrosio and Scott Mendel: Thank you for believing that I had a book inside me.

Lisa Rogak: I can say with 100 percent certainty that this book would not have happened without you. I don't have the attention span, mental capacity, or experience to write about myself at length, but you thought that I was interesting enough to warrant a book. Thanks also (I think?) for forcing me to dig up my earliest memories in our talks, which resembled hours of therapy . . . but all in the name of engaging the reader. Also, thank you for putting up with my absentmindedness.

Carl: Thank you for believing that I had a YouTube channel inside me.

Mike + Meghan: For all the advice you've given me in both dark and happy times.

Steven: For all our wild adventures.

Samcrac: For eating up hours of my day talking on the phone about YouTube nonsense.

Joshua D: Thanks for helping me bring ICE-T to life.

Chad: My lead mechanic and good friend, you have a lot more of my mistakes to fix.

Chris S: Thanks for not selling me those Tesla parts... Now look at you, Mr. BIG CEO!

John V: Your free labor has carried me to new heights.

Joey C: Thanks for the safety goggles. I have a lot less metal in my eyes these days.

Alex P: I'm glad I could help convince you to quit your job. Now look at you!

Phil: A phenomenal Tesla hacker who saved me from everything ten times over.

Khac and Gentian: My two best friends since eighth grade. Steel sharpens steel; hanging with you guys increases my IQ by ten points. Thanks for the laughs. We need to hang out more often.

Jim Jankowsky at the Charlton Group: Best. Boss. Ever. (That is, if you *have* to have a boss.) Thanks for giving me support when I told you that I wanted to bring a flooded Tesla back from the dead.

Phil Dimanche: My first friend and partner in crime at St. Mary's. Thank you, big brother.

Polaris Capital Management: Thanks for allowing me to work for you, and for listening to my crazy ideas and stories as well as for the fancy Christmas parties.

Asad and Ji: My partners in crime at one of the best work times in my life, thank you!

Leerink Swann: Thanks for giving me a shot at my first job in the financial field. I wasn't ready, but hands down it was the most fun I've ever had at a job, and the memories I had working there as a young IT guy were endless.

Peter Satchell: Maybe you already know.

Jojo from NY: You've been there since day one! Thanks for joining me!

Elon Musk: From one African to another, thanks for inspiring me.

YouTube: I mean, come on.

Leenda: Thank you for taking up an entire chapter in the book.

Krystle J: I'm only putting you in here so I can invoice you for it later.

Tavarish: By the time this book comes out, that McLaren better be done.

eBay Motors: A major sponsor at *Rich Rebuilds*, you guys helped me bring the V8 Tesla to life.

Squarespace and ShipStation: Two sponsors that have been with me for the long haul.

Simone Giertz: Thank you for helping me with my big break, and for allowing me to help you with one of your largest and most ambitious projects.

Vice/Motherboard: For being one of the first to share my story with the world.

The cockroach: I'm still ready when you are.

Elsevier: My first job out of school and in the corporate world, thanks for giving a young clueless nerd a shot.

Rachel Mulhern: Thanks for being understanding when I threw up in the server room.

Tuan Nguyen: You may not know this, but you were a huge influence for my humor today and one of the funniest guys I know.

Joe Rogan: Since the last time I was on your show, I wrote a whole book! Thanks for giving me a shot.

Billy Baker from the *Boston Globe*: You beat my door down till I answered.

Biscuit: Thanks for all the financial advice over the years.

Henry, Breanna, and Victoria: The best kids a father could ever ask for.

Roderick: My only sibling, thank you for supporting me, and watching all my videos, and spending all that time together on the phone talking about how crazy our family is.

Mom: Without you, there is no me. Thank you for fostering my love of cars.

Allison: Thank you for putting up with me and allowing me to live my dreams, also for your unwavering support over the years and your trust.

Lastly, to every one of my subscribers: Thank you for pressing that Subscribe button because you wanted to see more of my crazy projects.